PRAISE FOR *Permission*

"Elissa Altman's marvelous, passionate and charming new book, *Permission*, is going to breathe freedom into your life. It is a clarion call for writers to tell their hard, lifelong truth, no matter how many decades they have agreed to stay silent. Lies and cover-ups won't save you. This book just might."

—ANNE LAMOTT,
author of *Somehow*

"I can't think of a better book on the craft of memoir. Erudite, wise and deeply personal, *Permission* burrows into the complexity of telling our own stories. This is a masterclass."

—KATHERINE MAY,
author of *Wintering*

"With *Permission*, Elissa Altman has given us a profound and generous gift. She candidly addresses the slipperiest questions behind making art from life: Can I tell my story? What are the risks and rewards? How do I care for myself—and others—in the process? There are only a handful of books I recommend every time I teach, without fail, and *Permission* will be one of them. This insightful, empowering book should be on every writer's shelf."

—MAGGIE SMITH, author of
You Could Make This Place Beautiful

"The work of writing requires a kind of rigorous solitude. Within that solitude, voices emerge, at times whispering, at times shouting *what right? How dare you?* This wise and beautiful book is the perfect antidote. Writers, keep *Permission* by your side. It's excellent company, as is its author. A true gem."

—DANI SHAPIRO,
author of *Signal Fires*

"In this astonishingly beautiful book, Altman articulates the ethics of writing the truth about trauma as a means of survival. *Permission* is a necessary book for any writer with an urgent story they aren't sure they're allowed to tell, a road map to clarity and light."

—KATE CHRISTENSEN, author of
Welcome Home, Stranger

"Elissa Altman's glorious new book, *Permission*, will allow anyone with a tale to tell or a story to share to unlock the obstacles thwarting a full-throated pronouncement of their truths. *Permission* provides an astute understanding of what it means to own and embody our history and to express it with clarity, candor, and artistry."

—DEBBIE MILLMAN,
author of *Why Design Matters*

PERMISSION

PERMISSION

THE NEW MEMOIRIST
AND
THE COURAGE TO CREATE

Elissa Altman

GODINE • BOSTON

Published in 2025 by
GODINE
Boston, Massachusetts

Library of Congress Cataloging-in-Publication Data

Names: Altman, Elissa, author.
Title: Permission : the new memoirist and
the courage to create / Elissa Altman.
Description: [First edition]. | Boston : Godine, Publisher, [2025]
Identifiers: LCCN 2024027542 (print) | LCCN 2024027543 (ebook) | ISBN
9781567927634 (hardcover) | ISBN 9781567927641 (epub)
Subjects: LCSH: Autobiography—Authorship.
Classification: LCC CT25 .A47 2025 (print) | LCC
CT25 (ebook) | DDC 808.06/692—dc23/eng/20241217
LC record available at https://lccn.loc.gov/2024027542
LC ebook record available at https://lccn.loc.gov/2024027543

First Printing, 2025
Printed in the United States of America

For my students,
who teach me every day,
and for Linda Wells, with deepest bows

You may do this. I tell you, it is permitted.
Begin again the story of your life.

—JANE HIRSHFIELD

CONTENTS

Contents

Introduction

[THERE WAS A SECRET.]

I DID NOT know that it was a secret, and this not-knowing changed my world, tilted it on its axis, spun it like a top; it broke my life and broke my health and it broke my spirit. It threatened my marriage. I began to stutter the way I had as a child; it altered my creative course, took my humor, rendered me silent for almost a decade. It left me sleepless and afraid. It inflated my ego (the narcissism of self-preservation) and then burnt it to ash; it unraveled my understanding of love and tribe and the meaning of grace. Toward the end, when I could no longer do the things that breathe air and light into my days—I couldn't write or work, I couldn't play guitar, I couldn't feed or support myself or the woman I love, I couldn't care for my health or my spirit; these things are *gravy*, Raymond Carver might have said—and I came close enough to the edge to peer over it, the non-secret secret saved me.

There was no truth, in the end; *just memory and words*, the poet Victoria Chang wrote in *Dear Memory*.

Definition: *A non-secret secret.*

A story that everyone knows, and everyone hides. A story that everyone knows and pretends never happened. A story that everyone knows and then forgets with the passage of

time. A story that some people know and some people don't.
A story encased in shame, like a chrysalis. A story that defines
and traumatizes generations past and generations to come,
guts them, and requires utter allegiance to someone else's
truth.

Here is a story that had been spoken of daily in my childhood home; I heard it morning and night for almost eighteen years until I left for college and then during college, and again, when I returned home.

This story had been part of our daily household conversation, like the weather or the news. This story had always been there, like wallpaper. As a young child, I dunked spongy white bread soldiers into soft-cooked breakfast eggs while listening to it. I took my vitamins to it, napped to it, took baths to it, played Marco Polo in our building's concrete pool to it, got dressed for school to it, walked the dog with my father to it. Later, I had my first drink and smoked my first weed to it. I lost my virginity to it. The story followed me to college in Boston, where I argued about it with my mother on nightly phone calls and then heard it again during monthly visits with my father, while we strolled along the Charles River. When I graduated and came home from Boston to live in my mother's Manhattan apartment, the story woke me every morning and echoed in my ears as I got dressed for my first adult job as an editor across town, and again when I returned to the apartment, over Tiffany goblets of cheap Soave Bolla that I drank until I could no longer hear the story clearly, and its sorrow became muted and soft, and I was finally, finally able to sleep.

In the hands of my mother, this non-secret secret was weaponized, used as a bludgeon, and was proof of *a profound moral failing,* she said, *a peculiar kind of weakness.* An indication that my father—they were divorced by then—came from a home destroyed by a monster and was therefore inherently broken and, by extension (and because I was so much like him and even looked like him and loved him so much) so was I. Our lives were layered with pain, my mother said, *like a strudel from the bakery,* and not one strand of my DNA had gone untouched by it. For my father, a kind and sometimes violent man, the non-secret secret shaped his outlook, and was the foundation of every struggle he faced and tried to overcome—work failures, depressions, addictions, self-esteem as unsteady as a three-legged chair—and instead passed along to me as though abandonment was our genetic destiny, like height, build, and the texture of our hair.

This non-secret secret was our hide-glue, binding us together for the entirety of our lives, long after my father took his last breath, and even though not a single member of his own family —his sister, brother-in-law, nieces, nephews—ever spoke of it in public. Some of them just didn't know about it. For others, it was secreted away, like the Kennedy sister who spent her life in seclusion rather than cast a pall of shame over her beautiful, doomed family. It was only when he met the woman who would become his beloved partner for the last twenty years of his life that his sorrow transformed and he began to heal. They loved each other profoundly; it was just a coincidence that she happened to be a therapist specializing in trauma.

What happens when half a family is devastated by a tragic story, and the other half buries it?

Like my father, I carried the non-secret secret with me viscerally. It was the basis for every decision that my father made throughout the course of his life, and in the end, it was the story that changed everything I, too, thought about memory, shame, truth, permission, risk, writing, teaching, and making art.

Early on, writes Jayne Anne Phillips in her essay *Outlaw Heart,* writers were *awarded possession of a set of truths, enlisted to protect someone's version, yet we lived in the context of those stories and we understood the truth to shift.* And from the earliest days when I imagined that I might become a writer, this was the story that I knew I had to unravel, unpack, attempt to fathom. This was the story that I had to understand in order to keep, paraphrasing Phillips, *sorrow from being meaningless.*

I have been a teacher of memoir now for almost a decade, and every student who attends my workshops first introduces themselves, talks about where they are from and a bit about their background and what they are at work on in their writing lives. And then, without fail, almost every student says that there is something that they want to write about, that they *need* to write about. Yet: they can't. An impossibility. They would vaporize on the spot, even if this thing they need to write about has defined them and their worldviews, and even if all parties involved are long dead.

They reason with the gods: they'll make it fiction, they say, and that way no one will ever know what they're talking about. Or they'll hide it in poetry and disguise their story in a villanelle. They'll write it as a one-act play. They'll take a pseudonym. They'll joke about going into witness protection. Not one of these possibilities will work; when it comes to these crucial stories, they will be told and told slant, or told straight. Because they must be.

Every family has a core legend, a koan—a defining, foundational, sometimes cryptic narrative around which its generations are coiled. Left unresolved, it will pop relentlessly back to the surface like a rubber bath toy. It is the story that appears when we least expect it, in primary relationships both successful and failed, in parenthood, at work, in recovery meetings, in the patterns that our therapists tell us they see. It is an endless loop: a thin Möbius strip that vibrates like a guitar string.

This is mine: my paternal grandmother was a comely, frosted-haired, thick-browed, elfin woman who left her Central European country in 1900 when she was two; who cared for me and saved my life when I was deathly ill as a teenager; who padded across her linoleum-floored Coney Island kitchen in gold vinyl ballet-style slippers every morning and night; who had been a child prodigy making a Town Hall appearance playing Chopin when she was fourteen; who played half-and-a-dollar poker; who had a salty, ribald sense of humor; who loved to laugh; who had a tiny gambling addiction; who made a nice brisket and a decent chicken, and matzo balls as heavy as lead weights; who lit Sabbath candles every Friday night; and who, when my father was three and my aunt eight, almost a century ago, abandoned them.

My mother *was* right about one thing: this non-secret secret touched all of us through the generations, whether we hid it or not. No one escaped its epigenetic grasp. It formed and shaped us and altered our emotional landscapes, our outlooks, our sensibilities. When I was a young child in the seventies, growing up in a community where dour-faced neighbors walked our streets with Auschwitz and Dachau numbers tattooed on their forearms, I heard older Jews call Polish the *language of death* and Yiddish the *language of survival.* In our case, the lexicon of abandonment became the sound and rhythm we knew and still recognize today as familiar. The undertow of maternal rejection flowed through every conversation, every argument, every family gathering, every threat; if I acted out as a teenager, my mother threatened to leave like my grandmother had or to change the locks and throw all my possessions *down the incinerator.* My grandmother's leaving resulted in my father's lifelong insatiable need for security and love and sustenance, as it did mine. My grandmother's leaving resulted in my aunt's lifelong insatiable craving for perfection, beauty, and safety. My father metabolized his experience through the constant telling and retelling of the tale of his mother's leaving to me, like a myth, as if to make sense of it, and codify it.

No one else in our family spoke of this non-secret secret, but I inherited it and the need to make sense of it the way I inherited the color of my father's eyes, his sense of humor, his temper, his quickness to tears.

I was raised in postwar New York City in the late sixties and seventies. The movies of my childhood—*Oliver!*, *Chitty Chitty Bang Bang*, *Walkabout*—are all built upon abandonment narratives. Oliver Twist lives in Victorian orphanage squalor; in *Chitty Chitty Bang Bang*, a child catcher lures the town's children to their doom in a cave, where they will perish, long forgotten; *Walkabout*'s young brother and teenage sister are dumped in the Australian outback to fend for themselves by a trusted but psychopathic father who first deceives them, then tries to kill them, then kills himself. Of the three, *Chitty Chitty Bang Bang* most terrorized me when I was very young: the child-catcher character, created by Roald Dahl, was thought to be a riff on the Nazi

Lebensborn program, which, during the Second World War, kidnapped Aryan-looking non-German children to be raised as part of the Reich. Dahl turned the program upside down: in a nod to anti-Semitic tropes, the dark-haired child catcher, utilizing his massive nose as a weapon with which to sniff them out, kidnapped beautiful little blond children. Once lured into his prison-on-wheels with sweets and toys and various false kindnesses, the children, screaming for their parents, are locked up and sent to a cave beneath the town castle where they will live and die while the world goes on without them just above their heads; they are made to believe, in a twist that I only came to know as an adult is considered a form of psychological torture, that their parents have forgotten them and moved on with their lives.

But it was *Walkabout* that undid me and has stayed with me into adulthood, causing me countless nightmares involving one or both parents abandoning me in a barren place where I would surely die alone. This is the foundation of the Levitical story of Azazel, the scapegoat, who is made to shoulder the burden of its community's sins, walked out into the Sinai desert, and set free to wander alone forever. Early on, I believed that somehow the two children in *Walkabout*—a young boy and his older sister, almost the same ages as my father and aunt had been when my grandmother left—had merely been separated from their father on a trip to the Outback; this was terrifying enough, and exactly where my prepubescent brain went when I got lost in our local Queens department store while shopping with my mother. Fear of abandonment is primal, which is why small children who get separated from parents in stores are so terrorized by it. It's why nursery school drop-offs are so fraught for both children and their parents. When I was in college and saw the movie again in a Jungian psychology class, I came to understand that the story was not at all innocuous; it was about deception and doom and premeditated murder and the rapacious cruelty of untreated mental illness, social norms, the power of nature, and racism— the brother and sister are helped by a young Aboriginal teenage boy with whom they share no language.

I could metabolize the scenes of the brother and sister in the Outback, and even the violent hunting scenes. But what left me paralyzed with recognition was the idea of parental deception: the siblings are school children who live with their ordinary middle-class city parents like mine in an ordinary Sydney apartment building just like the one where I lived in New York. It was a relatable story, and not based on fantasy or whimsy, like *Chitty Chitty Bang Bang*. In *Walkabout*, the children were taken for a ride to a place of danger under false pretenses—a picnic, a con—as my family sometimes did, be it a terrifying doctor's appointment disguised as a trip to a toy store, or a violent, bloody spaghetti western that my father absolutely had to see, preceded by a string of Bugs Bunny cartoons. Through all of this, the sister in *Walkabout*—like my aunt—maintained a cool facade of steady, almost superhuman composure misaligned with the terrifying magnitude and physical and emotional violence of the situation.

My aunt never spoke in my presence of having been abandoned by her mother and at age eight taking charge of my three-year-old father's care when they were briefly put in an orphanage and then a foster home. She became a mother figure for my father—for the whole extended family, really—and made it her life's work to create a stable and loving environment for her husband, children, niece, and nephews. She likely instructed my father never to speak of it, and until he married my mother, he never did, although I am certain that he desperately wanted and needed to: it had been a seminal moment in his life that altered who he was and would be at the cellular level. Living with what we now recognize as complex PTSD, he eventually spent five days a week in Jungian analysis, trying to process what he had lived through as a child. After I was born, he could no longer stay quiet or contain himself. He sought release from his nightmare in the telling and retelling of it, and he made me the keeper of the story, even when I was in single digits.

Although she eventually returned, the trauma of having been abandoned by their mother was far-reaching, and while my aunt chose to conceal the experience in order to protect her family from the pain, my father made it a part of our daily conversation. In *Walkabout*, everything I knew to be true and feared more than anything was confirmed: children are abandoned and harmed by the people they love and trust most in the world, the people who are meant to care for them. *Possibility: a mother could go out for a manicure and not return. A Saturday night at the movies might result in an orphanage. It happened to my father, and it could happen to me.*

This was our non-secret secret.

⚜

I was in my forties—it took that long—when I began to ask the question: *why?* I was already writing essays and stories, and I wanted to know the truth.

Why did my grandmother leave? What did that day look like? How did she move through the hours after her decision? Why did she return? What had happened to make her want to leave?

Although she came home three years later, the damage was done. My father was three years old when she left and six when she returned; his need for stability, nurturing, and emotional sustenance manifested at the table in various unfulfilled cravings for the dishes that she'd made for him and only him—the Brinser cheese, the blintzes, the special European tea cakes he associated with love and security—and, as an adult, in the lusting after expensive things he could ill afford, like extravagant gifts for his sister and elderly parents, thousand dollar suits, the hottest new Hasselblad cameras that he had to have. Eventually, my father's addiction to pleasure, extravagance, and people pleasing would bankrupt him in his fifties, but I understood where it came from: he searched for beauty and safety as if the former begot the latter, wherever he could find it. When he died in 2002, I, his only child, began to piece together his story and the roots of my own like a tile mosaic. I unearthed boxes of cards and black-and-white scallop-edged photos, and short scribbles written twelve years after his mother's return; my father, by then a decorated naval officer in World War II and flying Grumman Hellcats off the deck of the *USS Enterprise* in the middle of the Pacific, wrote childlike rhyming poetry for her, begging her to never leave him again.

I do not blame my father for making his story my own. He had to tell it to make sense of it, to organize it, and it was fed to me like codependent pabulum. I knew the story like I knew what the backs of my hands looked like: it had been part of daily conversation in my childhood home. But my cousins, both significantly older than I, knew and *didn't know*; my aunt kept the story from most of them. In the same way that my father codified it by telling and retelling it, his sister—a stunning woman known for her meticulousness, who spoke five languages fluently, who traveled the world with her beloved husband, who was an ace golfer—chose to get on with her life, to cultivate joy and beauty for her children and grandchildren as though pleasure itself was a religion. In her home, the story of my grandmother's abandonment was buried; the fact that it was a secret was *also* hidden.

Our extended family holidays at my aunt's house were joyful, elaborate affairs around massive and ornate mahogany tables laden with cut crystal Waterford glasses and heirloom china and Irish linen and French burgundies. Warmhearted cousins and their children laughed, ate, drank, their manners perfect, while our grandmother, at the end of her life—her hearing aids whistling, her chin on her ample chest—fell asleep over her bowl of mushroom and barley soup. She was a walking contradiction, and I watched her closely: this little old lady who had left her children and who my mother called a *monster* for so many years, was now ancient, completely deaf, given to eruptions of spontaneous tears that left wide ribbons of grief coursing down her powdered cheeks. I knew her story because my father told it to me again and again with sorrow in his eyes, and my mother pulled it strategically from her back pocket like a switchblade during their fights—*Your mother never loved you,* she'd say, in the throes of an argument; *she left you.* During those formal family meals when she was in her nineties, I searched my grandmother's face for clues behind her terrible truth. I knew that she left; I wanted to know why.

Over the years, the story has been changed, edited, revised, altered like a game of telephone. Other versions—that it wasn't three years but four that she was gone; that it was my grandfather who left, not my grandmother—are not lies, even though census searches reveal that my aunt and father were indisputably living with my grandfather as boarders in someone else's home without my grandmother present as late as 1930. Attempts at concealing the truth were not ever nefarious, and what other family members believed were individual truths based on what they had been told, and told to cloak.

But I am my father's daughter, and I can only believe that

my father's version is the *empirical* truth; he told me not only the story of what happened to him and his sister but the story of how what happened made him *feel*. This is the version that I hang my hat on, and the one that makes the most sense to me. It explains our genetic code, carried through the generations: a pervasive fear of rejection, absolute devotion to family, a sense that the togetherness of the tribe overrides absolutely everything in its wake, the requirement of perfection.

Family is all, my father's sister once told me.

The greatest possible punishment, then, would be excision from and abandonment by the family.

No other emotion prompts secrecy like shame. I think here of psychologist Christopher Bollas's concept of the unthought known: when an event is so devastating that it cannot possibly be processed or comprehended by the mind, which clings to it and tries in vain to resolve it, only stripping its gears like an old engine.

As a writer, the non-secret secret that overwhelmed us for generations would forever alter my understanding of story ownership, shame, the choices we make in our creative lives, artistic strangling, the craft of writing, the morality of writing about someone else's pain, and, ultimately, the freedom to make art from personal history, be it yours or not.

In 2012, ten years after my father's death and twenty years after my grandmother's, I wrote a book that traced my own cravings and addiction to the table and relentless need for sustenance and safety to my father's fear of abandonment and my grandmother's leaving. My book was a simple love story—a linear narrative about meeting the woman who would become my wife after being single for a decade, coming out as queer later in life, at thirty-four, and moving from New York City to rural New England in the days before September 11. And in an eight-line paragraph toward the end of the book, I wrote of my grandmother's leaving, and her eventual return.

A year later, I would be tribeless. My grandmother abandoned her family; my family abandoned me.

A wedding in the Midwest: a joyful occasion. It was June. My youngest cousin, the handsome groom, shared our grandfather's—his great-grandfather's—name; I presented him with our grandfather's massive cantorial prayer shawl, which had been passed along to me by my father. I read words aloud about love, place, and devotion from Wendell Berry's "A Homecoming": *O love, / open. Show me / my country. Take me home.*

The rabbi wrapped our grandfather's shawl around the bride and groom's shoulders. The groom stepped on the glass. Another cousin leapt from his seat to gingerly collect the shards in a linen napkin and have them encased in a solid block of Lucite to preserve the moment when the glass shattered, symbolizing the fragility of life.

During the meal, I rose, wove through a throng of guests dancing to French gypsy jazz, exited the event space, and walked down a long, empty corridor to the bathroom. I heard high heels clacking on the linoleum, following me. A hand on my shoulder.

We did not give you permission to tell, a cousin said to me, as I turned around.

She was seething with anger; she backed me up against a cinderblock wall and checked to make sure we were alone, looking over her right shoulder and then her left. She bent down so that we were eye to eye and tapped her finger against my breastbone.

We did not give you permission—

We had loved each other very much. For a time, we'd been as close as sisters, and then, we weren't.

—but you did it anyway. We did not give you permission. It was not your story to tell. You don't own it.

I didn't breathe as she spoke, inches from my face.

We don't love you anymore, she said, and then she walked away.

Over the next decade, I was sliced out of my family for revealing in my first memoir the story of a young mother's likely excruciating decision to leave, which not only played a pivotal and crucial role in the book, but directly impacted the narrator—me—and the narrator's revelations about humanity, her worldview, and what it means to live through and heal from intergenerational trauma. I am who I am because of this story, and it could not have been left out without the narrative collapsing. After she returned, my grandmother spent the rest of her life as a pariah, as women who leave their children and husband often are. Although the story was not something that happened directly to the cousin who excised me from my family—or to me, for that matter—she had claimed psychic ownership of it. Her words spoken at the wedding rang in my ears, and they were familiar. I recognized them from the familiar grade school admonishments of my childhood:

Who do you think you are?

After our confrontation, I spent months trying to unravel what had happened. I could never have predicted it, and I offered heartfelt apologies for hurting people I deeply loved. My writing started to become freighted by questions of creative proprietorship, the ethics of writing about someone else, secrets, permission, and the shame that sits at their core. I was made to be dead: I was blocked by family all over social media. My wife and I were eliminated from every family event, large and small. We were relieved of our roles as godparents to a new baby in the family; we watched all the usual benchmarks—first Halloween, first day of nursery school, first day of grade school, arrival of a new baby brother who we would never meet and who would never know us—unfold on Facebook, as though we were lurking behind hedgerows. Our holidays were spent alone. In an act of finality, the family plot—my father, grandparents, aunt, uncle, and cousins are all buried there—was closed to me. During a random internet search, my father was shown to have no children. I had been canceled.

A close friend and author described it as *your own personal Holocaust; you woke up one morning, and everyone was gone.*

Telling my father's story not only impacted almost every part of my life and my writing—*what was I allowed to say? what did I have permission to tell? who owned the story?*—but it also changed how I thought about my role as a teacher of memoir. I could no longer talk about writing memoir without also unpacking the inevitable responses to it, be they justified or utterly absurd. A well-known memoirist friend of mine put it more succinctly when she said to me, *No one ever says, Yay! There's a memoirist in the family.*

In my case, shame coursed through the century-old story of abandonment like lava, and my father metabolized the shame not by *hiding it* the way his sister had done, but through the telling of it because he knew, *intuitively*, that light and truth dilute and ultimately render shame and destruction powerless. They obscure them, like an eclipse. He passed this knowing along to me, and now I pass it on to every writing student I have worked with over the last decade: handled with care, *light and truth move creatives to a place of compassion, humility, self-knowledge, and transcendence.*

PERMISSION

1

OWNERSHIP

*There will come a time when people
decide you've had enough of your grief,
and they'll try to take it away from you.*

—SARAH MANGUSO

I N 2002, shortly after my father died, I brought home from his house two ancient shopping bags containing many of his letters from his time in the navy, written in the forties when he was a night fighter pilot in the Pacific. My grandmother had kept them, and my father, her written responses to them; together, they comprised a conversation between an immigrant mother living in Brooklyn and her only son, a naval officer not yet twenty, flying planes in the dark off an aircraft carrier stationed somewhere in the middle of the vast ocean.

A bag of letters. A story of a mother and son. An arc of two lives bound together by love, circumstance, trauma, grief, the maternal.

Over the course of a decade, I read and reread my way through the letters, allowing myself to sink deeply inside another time and place and to get to know the ghosts of these two people: the teenager who would, in twenty years, become my beloved father, and my grandmother, who I didn't know well, but who had often been so vilified that rooms sometimes fell silent when she entered them. My father had kept the letters all those years, knowing that I, with no siblings, would eventually take possession of them. Still, I often felt like I was looking where I shouldn't, at memories and stories that were not mine.

And this is the conundrum that every memoirist faces when we begin to peel back the layers of truth and history. When Honor Moore was writing *The Bishop's Daughter*, she used as part of her research letters between her parents, her father's letters home from the war, her parents' letters to her, her letters to them, and her father's papers, which were in the archives of the

Episcopal Church. Before he died, Bishop Paul Moore had made sure that his daughter had access to correspondence that pointed to the fact of his bisexuality, which he himself had alluded to in *Presences*, his autobiography. Did Moore struggle with the question of ownership? Did she feel as though she was looking where she shouldn't?

For a brief period in the nineties, shortly after my grandmother died at ninety-three, I lived in her empty Brooklyn apartment near Coney Island, which she had shared with my grandfather, my father, and my aunt since 1933, right after my grandmother's return to the family. I was in my mid-twenties and had just gone through my first serious breakup—an illicit relationship with a woman that nobody knew about, so I had to grieve the loss alone even though I had to very publicly move out of our apartment—and had nowhere to live. My father, who continued to pay the $142-a-month rent on my grandmother's empty apartment long after she died, generously offered it to me for as long as I needed it.

I knew the apartment well because I had spent almost every Sunday of my childhood there visiting my elderly grandparents. When I moved in as an adult, nothing had changed: the tenants still dried their laundry on the lines strung between the fire escapes on a pulley system. None of the windows, which were original, had screens. The lobby, with its massive marble ornamental fireplace, was dark and dreary and smelled like industrial cleanser. My grandparents' apartment—the entire building— reeked of the food of a thousand Sabbaths. On the late January day in 1991 when I arrived there, the air in apartment 5H was still greasy with ancient chicken fat and the musty odor of doom. Many of the building's original tenants had lost family members who had chosen to stay behind in Europe, including my great-grandmother; tragedy of that magnitude has its own stench, and so stepping inside was like entering a time capsule that had been sealed for most of a century, shrouded in darkness.

When I arrived—brokenhearted, scared, poor, unsure of what my next step was going to be—I tried to unpack, but couldn't; the apartment had never been emptied. All of my grandparents' things still hung in the closets. The drawers in the bedroom bureau contained heavily starched and ironed shirts, blouses, and undergarments, many of them still wrapped in yellowing launderer's paper. In the medicine cabinet, I found my grandmother's Colgate tooth powder, her hairbrush along with her hair, a plastic container holding her dentures. Hanging from the showerhead, the enema bag that was never not there when I was a child. In the kitchen, the refrigerator was still on; a half-empty bottle of gefilte fish covered with wax paper held in place with a wide red rubber band sat on the top shelf. On the second: a container of margarine and a jar of damson preserves. On the end table next to the settee facing the television stood a box of Coffee Nips, its plastic seal ripped open. In the hallway closet were my father's letters home from the navy, which he would take once I moved out two years later, and which I would take when he died, a decade after that.

The day I moved in, it looked like my grandmother had just stepped out for a minute to run an errand. My father and aunt could not face their mother's death—she had left them just as she had done so many years earlier, only now she was never coming home—and so they kept her things exactly where they'd been for years, as though she might return at any moment.

I moved my books and papers into the tiny space that had

been my father and aunt's childhood bedroom, sat down at their little pine grade-school desk, opened up my notebook, and did the only thing I could do: I wrote. I filled journals; I wrote scores of essays; I wrote poetry; I wrote short fiction and began to make notes for a novel about an assimilated postwar family in New England trying and failing to leave their tragic past behind. None of the pieces were published—I didn't submit any of them—and it didn't matter. The apartment was suffused with stories of the past and a genetic memory that was as much mine as it was my father and aunt's. I began filling in the missing pieces of stories I'd heard for years; for the eighteen months that I lived there, I wrote to try and organize our story of love, abandonment, grief, hope, and profound forgiveness, searching gingerly for the corners and the edges as though I were looking for a foundation.

It is thirty-two years since I moved out of my grandmother's apartment, and twenty-four since my father died. I keep the letters in black archival files on the top shelf of my office closet, sorted and arranged by year and, whenever possible, because of the strict wartime censors, location. Every once in a while, I take them down and read through them again; as a writer who has spent a decade jigsaw-puzzling together this complicated family history based on stories molded and shaped and changed like in a game of telephone, the letters are a tether for me. An *underpinning*. They are also emblematic of the mutability of memory and the fact that the truth can be filtered and extruded by individual circumstance and experience, and still be very real to every person it touches, be it the same truth, or different ones.

The stories the letters tell have appeared, over the years, in my books and many of my essays. In *Treyf*, a memoir of assimilation and what it means to be a grandchild of immigrants with one foot in the modern world and one foot in the old, there is the story of my father gorging himself on forbidden pork at his officer's club; in the corresponding letter, he writes home from his airbase hospital, telling his mother, *It must have been something I ate.* In another, he pleads for his parents to be proud of him after he earns his wings: *Maybe now you'll feel a little pride in me. Please.*

And yet many of these stories have been massaged and sieved over the years by other members of the family, and new truths formed and shaped. *Take one tale, add sixty years to it, and it becomes something else.*

✧

That's not how it happened, says a family member.

The admonishments come swiftly when we talk about my father's navy stories.

You're wrong! I'm told when what I have written conflicts with the version they have decided is the real one.

Does it even matter what it says in the letters?

That's not what they meant! We know the truth! You don't get to tell them—

But I do, and I will because they directly involve me; I will unravel them, unpack them, parse them, and tell them, using my father's letters as a springboard.

Yet, these people—I love them; we are close—still insist that I have no right to tell them, because they are different versions from the stories they know.

Who owns family stories?

Who owns the right to tell them?

When they said, *You don't get to tell them,* what did they mean?

Are stories merely alternate versions of reality?

Words have power, and we bear responsibility for them.

Creative work—storytelling, be it written or visual or musical—is also a moral minefield; we step tentatively through thicket and thorn, unaware of impending explosions, and we are often blind to them when they happen, so buried are we in the work itself.

We are responsible for the quality of our vision; we have a say in the shaping of our sensibility. In the many thousand daily choices we make, we create ourselves and the voice with which we speak and work, writes poet Carolyn Forché. But with those choices and with that vision—no matter how mundane—come risk. All art-making requires that we step into the gap, and create in a place of moral tension.

Must artists ask permission—from families, cultures, from our own hearts and memories—to tell the stories of their own lives and the lives of their ancestors?

A cautionary tale I share with every one of my memoir students: human beings are heavily invested in being right. If you write a story that conflicts with the established party line, or a secret that nobody bothered to mention to you is a secret, you will very definitely hear about it, even if what you have done is simply told the truth as you know it to be. Especially if.

A creative cataclysm: a writer loses her family because of the revealing of an ancient narrative on which her own story swings like a gate. She becomes paralyzed. Will she ever write again? If I want to write about my grandmother and unpack the question that no one ever asked—*Why did she leave? Spousal abuse? Mental illness? An affair? What compelled her to return? Was she miserable for the rest of her life?*—who will grant me permission to do so? If I do not need artistic permission, do I need it spiritually? Psychically?

Is truth-telling always conditional?

The poet Mark Doty writes, *You cannot sing your ancestors' songs as they intended them to be sung, as they would have phrased them themselves. If you choose to sing them at all, you will betray your forebears, because you will never understand them as they'd wish to be understood.*

I consider motive, and questions of betrayal: Why did I *need* to tell this story of my grandmother leaving? I wanted to find the truth. I wanted to honor my grandmother, to try and give her back her voice, even though my version of it will likely betray hers because I can't possibly, as Mark Doty writes, *know* it; I can only imagine and interpret. I want to rescue the brokenhearted three-year-old boy who grew up to be my father, to understand his fear and self-loathing, his often violent temper, his love of the world; I want him to know that he was loved. I want to fathom why every one of my *own* narratives beyond those I write about my family is wrapped tightly around a nucleus of abandonment.

I want to make meaning out of these stories, and expose them to light.

We tell stories to do this very thing: to make meaning of our lives. My father's story is built on a foundation of rejection and survival, secret-keeping and a catastrophic myth of perfection. Unraveling the story brings order and resolution to a chaotic truth that has flowed through our gene pool like a raging river.

Chaos comes from the Greek word for *abyss*: it translates to *an emptiness that existed before the world came into being; a disorderly mass.* Chaos is the opposite, then, of order and understanding. In the writing process and through draft after draft, we actively seek clarity; we tighten the creative monocular on that which we are trying to truly see, until its edges are sharp, and its meaning becomes clear and the truth is revealed. Had I not hulled the layers of my grandmother and father's story of her departure and his abandonment—even though I can only conjecture why she left—I would never have understood who he was, why he moved through the world in the manner that he did, and how his worldview was passed along to me. Making art from chaos creates an environment ripe for understanding, revelation, and, ultimately but not always, healing. Humans are innately drawn to writing the hard things because we *become the stories we make.*

We are what we were told we were, wrote Doris Grumbach. *We believed what we heard from others about our appearance, our behavior, our choices, our opinions. We acted according to all their instructions. Rarely if ever did we think to look within for knowledge of ourselves. Were we afraid?*

Often, we are.

Who gets to tell a particular story? To craft it? To make it public? Is it an ethical question? A moral question? Is it a question of ego? We all know this person: the one who takes over a conversation that's already underway because his version of a story is, he feels, the only one. Again: humans are invested in being *right*, even when they aren't. This is how wars are started, be they in the bedroom, in the boardroom, in Congress, on the battlefield. Stories are inevitably owned; *I must be right, and you must*

be wrong, and I get to say whether you can tell the real story. In politics, it is called *controlling the narrative*, and in public relations vernacular, *spin.* Entire teams of people are assembled and paid for by governments and elected officials to control—to own—a narrative. At its most benign, spin is a game of *he said/she said.* At its most insidious, controlling the narrative can be weaponized in the most familiar and horrific of ways: The happy indigenous American who welcomed the Pilgrims. The happy slave who willingly submitted to their master in the American South. The Nazis knew this when they told their story that Jews had horns, or flat heads, or were vermin; they convinced enough people of the story, and the people believed them. The keepers of those well-crafted stories are never happy when the truth is finally revealed, at long last.

After experiencing abandonment because of writing a story about abandonment, I have finally come to understand what it is that makes our species so profoundly attached to permission and story ownership: it is a manifestation of control and creative hierarchy designed to keep people in their places with the threat of shaming, which is, perhaps, the most ancient and biblical of ways to keep people in their place, and is not to be confused with guilt. *Guilt,* according to Brené Brown, means *I did something bad*; shame means I *am* bad. What comes out of shame? Self-loathing, self-hatred, self-flagellation, the certainty that our creative lives are doomed because, if we're *that* bad, then why even bother. Shame says that we must hide ourselves, like Adam and Eve; shame caused our fall from the garden. Shame demands that we must hide our stories, and the very essence of who we are.

In her book *An Absorbing Errand,* Janna Malamud Smith writes that *shame heats up when you are perceived to be attempting,*

even silently desiring, to rise above your assigned caste or station—
when it appears you think more of yourself than others think of you.
She goes on: *The feeling may have evolved in part to stabilize social*
hierarchies of dominance and submission.

Some years ago, I had a new memoirist in my workshop who
had been, to that point, a writer of fiction because she said she
simply could not bear the possibility of being shamed if she upset
someone she loved by telling the truth. I told her, as I tell all my
students, that grappling with shame as a part of story ownership
and permission happens to every one of us, and simply changing
genre does not fix the situation. Instead, we have to recast the
idea of ownership so that it becomes less binary and no longer *I*
own this story and you don't.

If the stories we tell are *not* proprietary—if nobody claims to
be right and nobody claims to be wrong, and instead each of us is
just telling a story as they know it to be, without intent to harm
or persuade or compel or sway or exact revenge—then there's
no top dog, no leader, no grand pooh-bah, no one at the tip of
the familial totem pole directing what is allowed to be said and
what isn't. Buddhists lay down their swords instead of fighting,
and metaphorically speaking (and otherwise) it is a maddeningly
powerful act precisely because there is no winner, no battle for
place and power, and therefore no ability to shame. When I was
told during my cousin's wedding that I hadn't been given permission to write the story of my grandmother abandoning her
children, my cousin had anointed herself keeper of the story
keys. But the bigger issue was that I hadn't actually *asked* for
permission. Translated to ownership of story, writers of memoir
inevitably will be told that the stories are not ours to tell, or that
we've *gotten it wrong.* But if there is no right and no wrong, then
there is no leader, no one in charge of the party line, and any
sense of dominance collapses.

How might a writer handle it when told that they've gotten the story wrong and who do they think they are? By diffusing it rather than engaging in the Sturm und Drang of an argument that they will *never win*. Because an argument over who gets to tell a family story is rarely about the story itself; it is about power, shame, control, and fear.

I'm sorry you feel that way, we say when challenged with the binary wrong versus right, the finger shaken in the face. *But this is how I know the story to be.*

And then: we lay your swords down, wish them well, and walk away.

In ancient communities, the punishments for telling a secret story that one does not own—for breaking someone's rules of proscription, inadvertently or not—run the gamut from the cutting out of the truth-teller's tongue to stoning or banishment. In our modern day, we read similar stories coming out of certain communities and are familiar with them as being unthinkable, archaic responses to nominal offenses. In those cultures, the punishments are meant to defend the honor of the communities against words that were never meant to be spoken; they are called *honor killings*, and are common, too, among street gangs. *A fatwa.* Someone said something they weren't supposed to. Whatever the penalty—the tongue, the stoning, the caning, the banishment, the killing, an eye for an eye—the goal is the same: to silence the truth-teller and keep the secret—*the story*—a secret, lest the tribe, or the family, vaporize in a cloud of shame. To render the truth-teller dead. To warn others: *this is what happens if you dare tell the story you're not supposed to tell, and for which we will never give you permission.*

One of the most complicated components of writing memoir begins long before the first word is ever written, and it is disconnected from the practical craft and skill required to write well; I don't necessarily believe that everyone can learn the craft that will make them a great writer in the same way that I don't believe that everyone can learn the skill it takes to become a neurosurgeon or a concert pianist. When I am leading a memoir workshop, not everyone comes in at the same level, and not everyone leaves that way. But whomever they are, these are the questions that almost always come up first: *Who owns this thing that happened to me, that I must write about? If I am writing about something that happened to my family a century ago and all parties are long gone, why do I feel at best squirmy and uncomfortable, and at worst like shit when I write about it?*

There are many answers to these questions, but the most foundational is the intractable marriage of shame and power. Someone at some point—a sibling, a parent, a distant relative, clergy, a teacher, a movie producer, an entire culture—told you either directly through words or indirectly through actions that you were wrong, and that *this* was *the story.* No one ever told you that it was simply a version.

In the telling of my family's story—*a twenty-three-year-old immigrant and new wife walks out on her family one day and doesn't return for three years, and it impacts generations into the next century*—I revealed a deeper truth: my family was profoundly human and flawed after all. My aunt's attempt at metaphysically shellacking our story with a veneer of perfection had failed as revealed by her young niece. There had been a blip. After nearly a century of everyone toeing the party line, someone went off script. Then there was the primal component of the story: mothers don't leave their babies. There was the cultural certainty, drummed into the heads of Jewish children from the ancient days of the matriarchs and the patriarchs through the Spanish Expulsion of 1492 through the pogroms, and reinforced in midcentury, post-Holocaust Jewish homes everywhere: Jewish mothers are selfless and prize their children and families over everything else.

But perfection is a dangerous myth, a cloak woven of fears of inadequacy and ostracism and self-loathing; perfection *is* the emperor without the clothes. It demands that we be something other than who we are for the sake of someone else's reputation and cultural acceptance, both of which have nothing specifically to do with us. Perfection causes generational and systemic destruction and, in the words of Anne Lamott, *will keep you cramped and insane your whole life.* Telling the truth where false perfection once existed—casting shade and doubt on it—results in humanity, empathy, and compassion. And sometimes, trouble.

A year after my book came out in hardcover, the paperback edition was released. Before publication, I had the opportunity to remove the eight lines about my grandmother as a gesture of goodwill to the cousin who had sliced me out of the family. There were some other small changes that I did make out of deference to her. I also considered making the broader excisions, but I made a creative inquiry first: *Was the substory of abandonment even necessary to the book as a whole?* Could the narrative work without this fundamental, core truth that made my father who he was, and I who I am, or would it be transformed into a three-legged table?

The truth—my grandmother's, my father's, and mine—had to be told. The narrative could not stand without it; I left it in.

Did my cousin *own* the story of my grandmother's leaving? Was it hers, like a fingerprint?

No; we all own it.

When do we know that it's safe to write a story that involves another party? We can't possibly. Arguably, almost every story involves other parties. That said, I believe that story ownership is predicated on there being an unquestionable through line that runs from someone else's life directly into and around your own, ensnaring it: experience, separated by generation, decade, time, and place *can still be shared experience*, even if you never met the person you're writing about. The facts of intergenerational trauma are now scientifically indisputable; we carry them at the cellular level. But if we tell the truth about, for example, a family matriarch's heinous behavior to her Bavarian housekeeper in postwar Shaker Heights—something I witnessed as a young child at a nineteen sixties suburban Ohio cocktail party when the matriarch thought no one was looking—because it ground into the family fiber the unmistakable whiff of revenge, and we choose to write about it, we will, most certainly, hear from the surviving parties. When Honor Moore wrote about her late father, Bishop Paul Moore, revealing him to his community as bisexual, she was publicly pilloried in the Letters to the Editor section of *The New Yorker* by her siblings, who said it was not her story to tell; they felt that their father had gone to extraordinary lengths to hide the reality of his life, enlisting his children in the keeping of his secret.

Who the hell was she, and what right did his daughter have to reveal it when he was no longer around to defend himself? She had every right: Moore's papers were specifically left to her by her father, he had already published a memoir clearly implicating himself, and she had provided each of her siblings with a pre-publication galley so that they could comment on anything that made them uncomfortable. Only one did. Honor Moore herself identifies as bisexual (as did her maternal grandmother, painter Margarett Sargent, about whom she writes in her memoir *The White Blackbird*), and her life was indisputably and profoundly touched by her father's sexuality. Honor Moore could in no way write about or understand her own life without writing about his.

When we are directly touched by a story—meaning, we are *involved* in it, in its evolution—that story is, in part, ours. I could no sooner disengage myself from the story of my grandmother than I could change my height. In the aftermath of the excision from my family, I came to understand that her leaving was such an immense source of shame that it had been cloaked: younger family members were told that it was my grandfather who left because Jewish women don't abandon their children. They hewed to cultural stereotype: men leave, and women don't. A false narrative of maternal perfection was fashioned to throw the family's children off scent. What had been so dangerous about this story that had been shared around my childhood dinner table that writing about it caused my expulsion? What was at stake? It was the betrayal of a carefully constructed, century-old silence designed and arranged, as Victoria Chang writes, *like furniture.*

Over time and distance, when I allowed myself the space to talk about my excision, I began to speak with other creatives and writers—award-winning colleagues and friends whose work I deeply respected, and who had honed their craft over years of work, but also people who made art *purely for the sake of it*—and I learned: they too fought the battle of ownership and permission to tell the non-secret secrets and stories that defined them. The novelist and memoirist Dani Shapiro discovered in her late fifties that her biological father was not, in fact, the beloved man who raised her with Dani's mother in suburban New Jersey, and she had lived more than half a century believing her story. Why wouldn't she? She learned the truth many years after her parents died. The late naturalist, Barry Lopez, stepped out of genre and wrote a long-form essay that revealed his secret truth: he had been sexually abused as a child by a man who ran a sanitorium where a friend of his mother's was being treated for alcoholism. Lopez had carried the story with him for decades, like a stone in a pocket, turning it over and over; it was clarified and smoothed with the passage of time until it could finally be written, as he discusses in an interview with National Public Radio's Terry Gross, as a way to restore his self-worth and dignity, to claim ownership of his story, and *be taken at face-value and believed,* which is all any child ever wants.

Shapiro did not have to contend with her parents' responses to her discovery—a core question of her memoir *Inheritance* is did they know or didn't they—and the ramifications about ownership of the story and of the truth of who Dani is genetically, although questions abound regarding her pursuing a relationship with her now-elderly biological father, who she found shortly after taking the DNA test. Was it as much his story as hers? Who could claim ownership of it if he had chosen to hide it, or if her own parents chose not to disclose it to her? In fact: *this is the author's story.* It is not *only* her story, certainly, but in writing it from her point of view, through the lens of her experience in the aftermath of her discovery, she owns her portion of it: *It happened to her. She is the product of it.* She unraveled the story, strand by strand, like a mystery, until she came to comprehend as much as she possibly could about the actual truth surrounding the truth of her own being.

Lopez wrote his essay "Sliver of Sky" long after both his abuser and his mother were dead. In the essay, Lopez's mother finally reveals that she was aware of what was happening to her son when he was a little boy—*I know what happened,* she says—and it is never spoken of again. Lopez unpacks this story in a voice and manner that is journalistic; at the time of the writing, he was no longer the child he had once been. All parties were long gone. He had every right to write it, and he owned all of it. But if he had chosen to, he had every right to write it while they were still alive.

Write as though all parties are dead, Cheryl Strayed once wrote, in a conversation with Sari Botton in the *Rumpus.*

Why does an artist feel the need to reclaim ownership—to finally tell a story—after so many years? Because humans pull toward the truth like metal to magnet. Because to write about a traumatic childhood from the point of view of the adult who survived it is to step *back* into that time and place, to, as Jayne Anne Phillips writes, attempt to *intervene in the dynamics of loss.* Humans want clarity. We want to make sense of our lives. We want to *understand.* Some artists *also* seek revenge, and this is also where the questions of motivation and intent come in: before we even begin, we have to ask ourselves why we are so compelled to tell our stories, and if we're honest and the answer comes up *Because I want to get back at them,* we have to be honest with ourselves and examine that too.

In every workshop I lead, whether I like it or not, ownership and permission trump craft; they always come first because of their emotional primacy. They are the two elephants in the artist's room. At some point, someone or something has told us, *No, you may not tell this story,* and so we sit at our desks or work in our studios, chewing on our fingers and squirming under shrouds of humiliation for even wanting to create the art that gives meaning to our lives and reveals truths that invariably revolve around but are not limited to trauma, healing, sex, desire, and forbidden passions that come in all sizes and shapes and colors.

Tara Westover, author of *Educated*, and Jeanette Winterson, of *Why Be Happy When You Could Be Normal?* were made to choose between the devil-you-know traumatic oppression and gaslighting they grew up with and moving into a place of *freedom*, which was unknown to them. Westover was repeatedly gaslit over her desire for a better education than the one she was getting at the hands of her end-days father and doormat mother, who failed to protect her children. When she told her parents that she was being violently abused by an older brother, she was ostracized for speaking out against him. Ultimately, Westover wanted out: she wanted a future and an education, she wanted to live her own life and was forced, finally, to choose loyalty to herself and to her own story over loyalty to her family. Freedom aside, her choice was devastating: *My life was narrated for me by others,* she writes in *Educated. Their voices were forceful, emphatic, absolute. It had never occurred to me that my voice might be as strong as theirs.* Westover was still estranged from her family as of 2023, but at least one family member has had their own say: LaRee Westover,

Tara's mother, wrote her own version of the family story in 2020, entitled *Educating*.

In Jeanette Winterson's *Why Be Happy When You Could Be Normal?*, the author recounts her upbringing as the adopted child in a fundamentalist Christian family in England; growing up in an emotionally and physically repressive, abusive atmosphere, Winterson realizes that she is gay. She turns to writing as a life preserver: *I needed words because unhappy families are conspiracies of silence,* she writes. *The one who breaks the silence is never forgiven. He or she has to learn to forgive him or herself.*

The writing of memoir is often fraught; our friends, colleagues, families, entire cultures turn writers into pariahs for what we create, for who we are, for how we dare take ownership of our own stories. In writing memoir, some of my students became creatively blocked; it became impossible for them to work. Others somatized their creative paralysis and became physically unwell. After not being sick a day in my life, I became ill with every conceivable affliction for the better part of a decade following the ostracism from my family. Most of us suffered the invisible ravages of psychic exile, gave ourselves permission to grieve our losses, and then continued with our craft. Because if someone has gone to the trouble of disowning you, it's important to remember: you cannot be disowned twice.

Beyond time, space, and money to write, permission is the single biggest hurdle that the creative—new or accomplished—faces, and often over the most mundane of issues. In the workshops I lead, every writer who shares with me their experience of being petrified by the prospect of telling a story they weren't meant to tell has one thing in common: a primal fear of ostracism so visceral that it obscures the importance of the art-making itself.

Rilke, in *Letters to a Young Poet*, writes, *The work of the eyes is done. Go now and do the heart-work on the images imprisoned in you.* The non-secret secret I wrote of lashed me to the mast of my own creative truth, my eyes opened wide. I was faced with a choice: never write about my grandmother again and live a creative life built on an intergenerational sin of omission until it began to craze like fine porcelain, or excavate the truth—our truth, my truth—and our story to somehow find clarity, beauty, bravery, and the utter humanity in it, and also find compassion for a grandmother who died when I was in my early twenties, who paved her family's road with the stones of abandonment, pain, addiction, and the myth of perfection, and in doing so, finally come to peace with it.

I would choose the latter.

∽❧∼

Storytelling is what humans *do*; we are hardwired for it. This is also something that I say to my students in every workshop I lead when, inevitably, they tell me that they can't possibly write the story they need to write—that they *have* to write—and that has brought them to my workshops.

If you cannot write the thing that brought you here, then why are you even here? I ask.

They look at me sheepishly. In some cases—many cases—there are tears.

Because this is my story, they say. *I am who I am because of it.*

They understand the risks; truth often outweighs them.

Every one of us is the carrier of many truths. We can only speak from our own experiences, our own points of view, and the filters through which we see the world. No one owns the right to craft *our* story but us, but we must remember that the complex work of memoir demands that we also write with clarity, compassion, and ambiguity, which allows the reader to determine their own response to the story. Will there be unexpected reactions and responses to what we write?

Again, as Mark Doty wrote, *You cannot sing your ancestors' songs as they intended them to be sung, as they would have phrased them themselves.* Will there be fallout? Always. It can never be predicted or projected, and that is one of the few absolute truths that each of us faces, whether we are award-winning writers with five books under our belts or just starting out, sitting down at our desks with an open notebook in front of us, waiting for the first line.

2

A GIFT UNBIDDEN

To accept the fruits of these things as gifts is to acknowledge that we are not their owners or masters, that we are, if anything, their servants, their ministers.

—LEWIS HYDE

THE NEED to tell a story—to write it, paint it, sing it, shape it out of clay, cook it—often feels dire.

My father's desire to tell the story of his childhood was all-encompassing; trauma, coupled with shame and fear, resulted in a psychic stranglehold on it. He was very definitely warned against writing or talking about it under the threat of further emotional abandonment. I wrote about it instead, and by then he was a decade gone and unable to witness its ramifications: like him, I was abandoned. The story he could not tell was the story I had to.

Students come to my workshop burning with the need to write about *The Thing That Happened to Them* and *To Tell Their Story.* They begin with a particular urgency, as though they've been shot out of a cannon. Their bodies are pitched forward as if they're about to share a secret; they lean in and whisper, *I have a great story, and I really need to write it.*

What is it about? I ask. Often, they can't say, exactly, beyond *This thing happened and I need to tell it.*

They arrive with two hundred pages; they've squirrelled away time, awakened early while their children are still asleep, hid out in a conference room during lunch at their corporate day jobs or the laundry closet when their mother for whom they are caregiving is napping, or they've locked themselves in the employee bathroom at Home Depot, where they work mixing paint; they write whenever they have a moment because this story *will not wait.*

Wallace Stevens wrote out his poems at night after composing them on his morning walk to his day job in a Hartford, Connecticut, insurance business. Kathryn Harrison wrote her first novel in part while she and her family were driving to a Maine vacation house, often writing while she was driving. The late humorist David Rakoff, a friend and colleague of mine, wrote whenever he was not at his job at HarperCollins. Toni Morrison wrote every day in the predawn hours, having made herself a cup of coffee while it was still dark; she credited her children for putting her on that schedule, which became what she called her preparation to enter a creative space *that I can only call nonsecular.*

When my students arrive in class, they often cannot stop thinking about *the thing they must tell*; they write like their hair is on fire. And then, when they *do* stop for a breath, they realize that there are complications: the elderly parent who doesn't want The Thing to be written about; the threatening spouse who is fighting for custody of the child, just because they can; the deep-seated guilt for toe-dipping into the story that generations have made it a point to hide; the distant cousin you see only at weddings and funerals who will say *that never happened* and call you a liar, and just like that, your days of going to Thanksgiving dinner are over. We are drawn to the creative act—of making meaning out of chaos—and the most ideal creative experience that any of us ever have is *art-making-as-compulsion*. The necessity to create takes over. And yet we still must face the naysayers, and we have to make a decision. *Do we create, or don't we?*

I was speaking at a workshop on memoir and permission when someone in the audience raised their hand to ask a question about a book that I had written about my relationship with my mother.

How did you allow yourself to write about your mother while she was still alive? they asked. *How could you face yourself every morning?*

Because, I said, *I had to approach the work from the point of it being a gift. I wasn't writing to seek revenge against my mother's cruelties; I wasn't writing to emotionally maim. I was writing to understand, to come to a place of revelation and clarity and, if at all possible, healing and transcendence.* After a lifetime of enmity, perhaps we would both come away with understanding and a sense of peace; that is exactly what happened.

But was the same true for the story of my grandmother? Was losing half of my family in any way a gift? It was the most extraordinarily painful, frustrating, devastating, excruciating, traumatic experience of my life. And yet it *was* a gift. Telling the truth about where we all came from—that the narrative of abandonment was our intergenerational story—was illuminating and revelatory. To this day, more than a decade after my memoir's publication, I still pour obsessively over texts dissecting the Azazel story in Leviticus and theories of family scapegoating abuse (FSA), first identified by psychotherapist Rebecca C. Mandeville, and I have traced those patterns back generations. The truths that emerged from telling the story of my grandmother's leaving were apocalyptic.

And while it is impossible for us to control how our work will be received by the people who appear in it, we must still approach it and them with no small amount of empathy. *For the drama to deepen, we need to see the loneliness of the monster and the cunning of the innocent,* wrote Vivian Gornick.

Translated to one's writing life, that state of creative flow that feels almost preternatural is elusive, like dark magic. In the throes of creating a story I must tell, there is urgency, but there is also trepidation. The more I try to avoid it, the more I must do the thing that will be an expression of the story I want to tell, to make order out of the tumultuous world around me. This is the creative monkey on my back. A compulsion that I recognize from another creative part of my life as a secret, private musician of more than fifty years.

I told no one about the place and importance of music in my life because I was not the officially designated musician in my family. That role belonged to my late younger cousin Harris— my beloved playing partner from the time he was a child until his death in 2008.

My colleagues didn't know I had played the guitar since I was four and studied with Paul Simon's brother; my friends had no idea. I wanted the fact to be mine, just mine. I did not want it to become fraught; I didn't want it to be examined under a psychic microscope. I didn't want it to be up for grabs or somehow taken away from me. I didn't want to have to make excuses for it; I didn't want it hauled out at parties.

But, in the nineties, when I lived in Manhattan, I often played guitar for hours at a time; it was not something I necessarily *intended* to do, but it became rote. I would often take my Martin out of its case at six in the evening and look up again at ten, realizing that I hadn't eaten dinner, or done reading I'd brought home from work, or fed my cats. This was my *flow state*— that creative meditational place where distraction simply does not exist, and I was one with the guitar. At the end of a writer's workshop in upstate New York where I was teaching with poet Carolyn Forché and the late *Los Angeles Times* food writer

Jonathan Gold, and where I had been leading a weekend class on truth in the memoir process, a teaching assistant handed me their old nineteen thirties Gibson acoustic, battered and beaten with time. I thought no one was listening, so I sat down in a corner and played it; someone came over with a fiddle, and we played together for an hour or so. I returned the guitar to its owner, and one of the other writers, an Iranian poet, turned to me and said, *You're a musician; you talk to God.*

What did she mean? I take it this way: with the making of art—any art—comes order.

In the seventies, I attended a sleepaway camp in northeastern Pennsylvania for eight summers. People who went there generally returned year after year; many started as young children whose parents sent them away from their homes in the city or the sub-urbs to make brightly colored lanyards and play tennis for eight weeks. Eventually, those children—I was one of them—became preteens, and then young adults, and finally counselors in charge of the next generation. Every summer ended with Olympics that split the camp in half into two teams of one hundred kids, who competed against each other fiercely for the better part of a week. Even now, I can close my eyes and recall the 1976 softball game where I made a triple play; I was thirteen. I remember the 1974 rope burning activity—each team had to build a fire tall enough to burn a rope strung between two eight-foot metal poles. I re-member the 1982 track meet where one of my eight-year-old girls—I was a counselor by then—dropped the baton halfway around the track, fell trying to pick it up, managed to grab it, and ran so fast to the finish line that she overtook the leader and won. Eventually, everyone aged out of camp and got too old to attend, even as counselors. Some bought equity in the camp so that they could continue to work there every summer into their seventies and eighties. A fair number of well-known people attended this camp, including the writer Geneen Roth, actor Hank Azaria, choreographer Jerome Robbins, and Michel Bourgeois, son of artist Louise Bourgeois. Most of us are still so connected to the place that we can't let go of it, even now. We attend each other's weddings and birthday parties, some of us vacation together, and my charges from 1982—now in their forties—have their own kids going off to college.

So when someone from my age-group passed away after a lifetime of ill-health, most of us dropped what we were doing— we're business professionals, parents and grandparents, authors, doctors, teachers, actors, people busy with our lives—and turned around as if in slow motion and looked backward at the fact of our friend, who had died. We gaped at each other, suddenly aware of our own mortality. We looked long and hard into the past, at who we were during those long summers in rural Pennsylvania. Most of us had lost touch with this man, our friend who had died; he had a serious condition that rendered him a perpetual outsider at camp—he had always been frail and gangly, his pallor a light gray. In an extremely athletic camp, where prowess on the field was an acceptable alternative to popularity, he was not an athlete. He was not a singer or a performer in the weekly camp plays. What he was, though, was a watcher, an observer, a witness. A sponge.

In his later years, confined to his home by illness and physical limitation, he took to re-creating—in writing—the Olympic events that had taken place fifty years earlier, down to the most minute details, including the weather, and shared them with us on the camp's blog. The rest of us traveled through our lives numbed by busyness, by the treadmill that we run on day in and day out. But when Bobby died, we dropped what we were doing and looked at the memories he had compiled—because they were our memories too—as though we were going back in time to a place where we were wholly different versions of who and what we would eventually become as we were hardened and changed by life. Susan Sontag wrote that a writer *is someone who pays attention to the world*; my camp friend had done just that and given us a gift unbidden, born of observance and memory and story.

We did not ask for it, but here it was.

I have seen far too much, a student of mine once said while trying to excavate a narrative at the core of her memoir. Without the telling of this particularly traumatic part of the story, the memoir would have fallen apart. The trauma was at its center—it was the pulsing cord around which the memoir was wrapped—and my student had to give herself permission to even *think* about it, much less talk or write about it. She had to step back from it and observe *The Thing That Happened* in order to craft her memoir with clarity, without cynicism or sentimentality, and in its most complete form. She knew that this was something she had to do if she was going to write this story—*to insist that sorrow not be meaningless,* as Jayne Anne Phillips wrote—she had lived through, which is why she had taken my workshop.

There were daunting but common issues my student would face: the dangers of retraumatizing herself, concerns that she would hurt the people around her who had lived through the experiences with her and chose to bury them, concerns that she would be called a fabricator by those who would want to discredit her memory. There was also the question of fairness: is it fair to write a difficult story involving one's own personal monster if that monster is now a frail older person with dementia?

Her story, which had haunted her and shown up furtively in one form or another in everything she wrote (she is a poet as well as a writer of narrative), became the engine of her own recovery, and by that I don't mean from substance abuse; it afforded her the ability to recover the creative parts of her story that were stuck in time and place and memory, as a result of *The Thing That Happened*. The thing she saw. The thing that she carried in her heart and her viscera, and ultimately had to write about to organize the grief she wore at the cellular level.

Writing became both the key and the lock; it was the vehicle for her healing. It gave her agency. And unless she chose to write about it, this thing that had haunted her for so long, her work and her creative life would never lead to a place of transcendence. It was a gift unbidden.

It is counterintuitive to imagine this as a gift, but *seeing*— having one's eyes opened in a way that perhaps others' eyes are not—is how we free ourselves from the strictures of shame, of secret, of the silent compact that entire cultures depend upon for keeping communities repressed and in their place, year after year, century after century. Our tidy little families with our petty little secrets and generations of lies that get carried across the years: we are a microcosm of those cultures and what they do, and if we want to exist in our families and our cultures safely, we must sign a psychic agreement that says, *No, I didn't see it. It never happened. Ignore the children in the cages. Grandad never got drunk and took a belt to his little boy who would grow up to be your abusive father. Grandma never walked out; she never left. She was a perfect mother, and we are a perfect people.*

But the minute we begin to observe the story and tell the truth, and we are moved to create art based on that truth and that observance—*it will not leave us alone*—we have been given a vital gift both creative and spiritual, whether we asked for it or not. Zora Neale Hurston had it right: *The force from somewhere in Space which commands you to write in the first place, gives you no choice. You take up the pen when you are told, and write what is commanded.*

Apply this to any creative endeavor: we take up the guitar and play what is commanded, or paint the painting, or throw the pot, or write the poem, or make meaning from our story of abandonment. The command gives us no choice; we cannot ask permission or wait on the decision of another party who might or might not grant us the time we need to create with dire urgency.

To ignore the command is to turn away grace. To accept it is a profound act of humanity, no matter what it brings with it.

3

OPENING MEMORY

*What good stories deal with is the horror
and incomprehensibility of time, the dark
encroachment of old catastrophes.*

—JOY WILLIAMS

I WAS A nervous, taciturn child, so completely possessed by the possibility that a mother could go out to an afternoon matinee and simply not come back that separation anxiety ruled my life far longer and more intensely than it should have, even as an adult. The abandonment theme is my koan, my life story, wrapped around my worldview like a snake. Dolly Parton's hit song "To Daddy," where the child narrator wakes to find a note saying that her mother has left, sends me into a queasy tailspin even now, in my fifties. When Laura Brown, the suicidal postwar American housewife who, in the movie version of Michael Cunningham's *The Hours*, leaves her young son Richie with a babysitter to spend the afternoon in a hotel room in which she intends to kill herself, her child's shrieks of *come back* as she drives away are bloodcurdling; he knows, intuitively, what her plans are. We learn, at the end of the story, that Laura Brown did abandon her family after all, and her son, who has grown up to be an award-winning poet dying of AIDS, has dedicated his abbreviated life to metabolizing the fact of her leaving on the page, in both his poetry and his fiction. It's a story—a truth—that he cannot stop telling, like a chronic hand-washer, and like my father.

Every writer is a subversive, whether we believe ourselves to be or not; every painter, every photographer, every artist who creates something from nothing is, in the doing, a truth-teller. When James Baldwin wrote, *Every writer has only one tale to tell, and he has to find a way of telling it until the meaning becomes clearer and clearer, until the story becomes at once more narrow and larger, more and more precise, more and more reverberating,* he did so with the knowledge that clarity often travels hand in hand with *perceived subversion*: they intersect. We write to unravel our narratives, to define them and our place in them. We write to tighten the aperture on our lives. And unless we live in a nunnery or a cave—and not even then—our stories are invariably and inescapably intertwined and coiled around the stories and memories of others.

If writers write because we want to get to the core of the truth, we will almost always have to face the fact that we will not only turn over the apple cart; we will often set it ablaze.

Women who leave their children are made into pariahs; Doris Lessing left two of her three children in Rhodesia when she left to pursue a writing life in London, and she was vilified. In Elena Ferrante's *The Lost Daughter*, the character of Leda leaves her young daughters for three years because, as Anna Solomon examines in her essay "Are You My Mother?"—which appeared in the *Millions*—the character says, *I loved them too much and it seemed to me that love for them would keep me from becoming myself.* Like my father, whose obsessive recounting of the tale of his abandonment in the most banal of settings (dinner table, dog walks, dropping me off at a friend's house on the weekend) was an attempt to organize a grief that could not be contained, I played the role of his best friend and confidante, even when I was in single digits. His often violent and unpredictable temper eventually mutated during the telling—he emptied his memory like an overstuffed change purse; he laughed and cried and struck and cried and laughed—and it was only fifty years later that I came to understand the truth after so much therapy that

I considered going to Lourdes if the couch stopped working: in being the recipient of his tale of maternal abandonment, I had also become his *replacement-mother*, his prepubescent, codependent sponge, and his comfort, ultimately left to sort out the facts and fallout of his abandonment long after he died.

But, as a childless woman and a writer who has devoted my professional life to my work, I was far less interested in the apparent ruthlessness of my grandmother's decision, and instead I searched for the answers to questions that no one seemed to be asking: *Was she in love with another man? A woman? Had she been beaten by my grandfather? Was she pregnant with another man's child? Was she separated from the music that, before she married, gave her life meaning?* I wanted to understand the truth—the story of why—because it is the humanizing piece of the myth that everyone glosses over. I came to understand that my family's rage against me had nothing to do with my grandmother's leaving and everything to do with the *shame of possibility* that she left in her wake.

It is easy to write someone as a one-dimensional villain, but in fact, every one of us and every story we carry is a complex plaiting. The truth of our stories is insidious. No one is all good or all bad, with the possible exception of some politicians, and not always then.

In revealing the story of my grandmother's leaving, I was searching for patterns of meaning, which is what memoirists do. I gave myself permission to write about my grandmother's leaving because, although I was born almost forty years after she left, the truth of her abandonment *is as much my story* as it was my father's. This is an exercise in epigenetics: it made my father who he was, and me, who I am. He searched endlessly for sustenance and safety; he searched endlessly for his tribe. My writing hinges on that story. My cousin-the-painter makes beautiful oil paintings of houses and gardens in full bloom: tidy, well-landscaped containers of lives, evidence of security and safety, places where abandonment is not part of the fabric of life. Her mother buried the story and didn't want it told, but, as stories always do, it came out anyway, with a life, a blood type, and a pulse all its own.

4

THE CHOICE TO CREATE

*I have come to believe over and over again
that what is most important to me must be
spoken, made verbal and shared, even at the
risk of having it bruised or misunderstood.*

—AUDRE LORDE

W E ARE the storytelling species; we make art to metabolize and clarify experience, to find the truth, to make meaning.

We are the crafters and sharers of narrative. We are the yarn-spinners and the myth-makers, the truth-tellers, the searchers. We write, we paint, we sculpt, we sing, we make music to make sense of our lives and to create order where there is disorder. As Robert Macfarlane writes in *Underland*, it was the earliest humans who held their hands up against the wall of a cave in Spain and spat out a mouthful of red ochre dust to form a handprint that said, This is my story. I was here. Remember me.

Our stories bump up against the stories of others. Unless we are living in seclusion, or in a nunnery, or in a cave on a mountain in Tibet, our lives are inevitably intertwined and linked: they overlap like the intersection on a Venn diagram. *Interdependence* is defined by the Buddhists as *being profoundly connected*, and it is the nature of reality, and of human life. None of us lives in a vacuum; our existence overlaps with and depends upon the existence of others.

If it is human nature to mold and shape the truth, then what is the difference between truth and fact? How do they touch issues of ownership and permission? The psychiatrist and trauma expert Bessel van der Kolk spoke on Krista Tippett's *On Being* about the concept of *individual truth*: put five adult siblings around a table and ask them what happened on Christmas in 1978 when Daddy got drunk on the Jim Beam, and they'll all tell you a different version of the story, including *Daddy didn't drink*. Each of those is a version of the truth as seen through the lens of each siblings' experience, and each is therefore valid, but there can be only one empirical fact. Siblings will fight tooth and nail to prove that their truth is *the* truth, and the only real (and therefore valid) one. But truth is *always* filtered through the passage of time, through one's eyes, through one's worldview. In 2017, when Donald Trump was a newly elected American president and millions of women converged on Washington, DC, to protest, he is reported to have gazed out the window at a vast sea of pink hats, enthralled at all the women who were there, he believed, to celebrate and adore him. This was *his* truth, despite the veracity of the situation: the empirical *fact* was that they were there as an act of enraged dissent, not celebration. Still: a filter is a filter, whether we agree with what it shows or we don't.

The act of writing memoir or personal narrative can be terrifying, and—I am sorry to say—these feelings do not ever abate; at best, we learn to live with them, cope with them, excavate them, metabolize them. It is understood, although rarely elucidated (except quietly, in whispered hushes, and mostly in therapists' offices), that much of the fear of writing memoir has to do with warnings so ancient that they have become embedded in our psyches. We might be called a liar, a fabricator, a falsifier-of-the-truth. We may be told that the personal essay we've written comes from a grudge: you really hated that third cousin once removed, and so you've decided to tell the story about why she was sent away for a while when you were teenagers. We may be told that it's just about revenge: your mother was so hideously cruel to you that you've decided to write about her so that everyone knows she's not the perfect church lady everyone thinks she is, and now she's too old to fight back. Or that abusive guy you were briefly involved with in the nineties is going to show up again in a dream sequence involving his getting drunk at an office party, and even though you've changed his name, likeness, and job, he will likely recognize himself. After writing her (then) shocking and revelatory memoir about her relationship with J. D. Salinger, *At Home in the World*, Joyce Maynard was called everything from self-absorbed to a hanger-on to (in the *Washington Post*) *incredibly stupid*, in spite of Salinger's withering and predatory treatment of his former student, who, in 1972, left a full scholarship at Yale as a freshman to live with him when she was eighteen and he, fifty-three. When Paul Theroux documented his friendship-gone-sour with his mentor, V. S. Naipaul, it was said to not be revenge, but just an examination of the arc of a literary friendship. Maynard, however, made the choice to tell her story and received—and continues to receive—so much vitriol over the book that she, in her own words, *might as well have killed Holden Caulfield himself.*

But whoever we are and however seasoned we are in the work we do, a large component of this fear of writing comes from shame. Together, fear and shame will conspire to quash creativity at every step, and they will, if we allow them to. How do fear and shame play a role in making the choice to write? What happens if we ask permission to write a particular story and that permission is denied? (Imagine this scenario: *Dear X: May I write a memoir documenting your abusive treatment of me as a child?*) How many vital stories are *not* being told—memoirs written, movies made, art made, souls healed—because of fear and shame?

And yet, the issue of creative permission and the stories we must tell is a tentacled moving target. Did Sally Mann have permission to famously photograph her young children un-clothed, in the name of art? Her children—Emmett, Jessie, and

Virginia—were photographed by their mother, as one journalist said, with *lapidary beauty*. The photographs created a firestorm of opinion, which continues to this day. In an interview upon the publication of her memoir *Hold Still*, she cited context: *When I was immersed in motherhood and saw my children running naked every day, I found nothing unusual or unsettling about it, but can now, decades away from that time, understand how someone not so immersed might. Without the context of our very private farm and the protection of the cliffs and the river, the pictures would never have been taken, I'm sure of that. And that is why it was so under-standably hard for some viewers to understand the work—they had to know about the context.*

Anyone who has spent any time in the rural shelter of a small country farm with no one around for miles has likely seen the carefree romping of young children who, depending upon the context, may or may not be clothed. This, however, is not at question, at least not as I see it: every one of us who has been to a beach or to a city park with a sprinkler has seen little ones running around in gleeful freedom and delight before being wrapped up in towels, whereupon they almost instantly fall asleep. Many of us have either photographed or been photographed as very young children in bathtubs, or baby pools, or on the beach on a hot summer day, all of which are (we hope) acts of innocent affection. Likewise, Mann's children were apparently used to their mother photographing them all the time, clothed and unclothed. The question is *not* about whether she should have photographed them, but whether or not she should have published those photographs before her children were of age to give their approval, or not. I remain on the fence; context always matters. I have no children, but I am also the survivor of child sexual trauma, and I turn into the Hulk if I have the sense that a child is in danger of any kind. I also believe that Sally Mann is a magnificent photographer and visual storyteller who deeply loved her kids. She could have waited to publish the photos; in my opinion, the rules change when it comes to children who cannot say no.

Where else does permission figure in in a world where artists can be canceled, their work tossed into the dustbin of history for their (sometimes horrible) actions? Do I have permission to still *publicly* love the work of poet Derek Walcott, even after accusations of sexual impropriety against him dating from the time he was a professor at Harvard University and at my own alma mater, Boston University, where he was renowned long before the cases were brought against him for parading in the nude, and worse, in front of the massive window of his brownstone overlooking Bay State Road in Boston? Do I have permission to watch *Annie Hall*, Woody Allen's masterpiece, and still consider it one of the finest movies to come out of the modern American film canon, even though he may be a monster? Closer to home, a neighbor of my childhood was thought to be a *perfect example*—pillar of her community, mother, expert party thrower, bank president—and every one of us wanted to be her or be like her when we grew up. How many of us got a glimpse of what a sadistic, alcoholic horror she was to her children when the garage door came down and the casserole went into the oven? Who among us has permission to tell *that story*? To tell *that* truth?

These questions hound me; as a teacher of memoir, I am faced with versions of them in every workshop I lead, when a writer says, *I want to tell this particular story; it's been haunting me for years and I have been writing it for years, but what gives me the right?* I answer them: *If this particular story touched you directly, you have every right to write it.* To be *so* compelled to write a certain story—to mine it, excavate it, unravel it, clarify it, hold it up to the light and turn it around like a prism—is an act of incalculable bravery. There are pitfalls and hazards everywhere.

There is creative growth and transcendence when we sit with the discomfort that arises from being the truth-teller and the artist. We acknowledge it, feel it, then cast it off and overcome the fear and the shame that we are often faced with.

Janna Malamud Smith writes in *An Absorbing Errand* that creative fear and worry can come in every shape and permutation and from many root causes: It might come from disloyalty to your family of origin, who may see you as besting them. It might come from the fact that creative expression beyond the confines of your childhood crayons and coloring book is alien to them. It might come from fear of ridicule and disapproval—fear that you might make a fool of yourself in the eyes of your community and that ridicule might be projected onto the people you love. Smith calls discovering and following one's creative impulse *finding the latch,* and she goes on to say that *finding the latch is not simply about choosing something to work at; it's about agreeing to enter into a complicated psychological space filled with ricocheting emotions.*

All those lovely and atmospheric pictures of writers on Instagram and TikTok? I tell this to my students: they aren't real. They don't necessarily show the truth, the fear, the worry, the lost sleep over whether one is making the right choice: to tell the story now, or to wait until all parties are dead, or to not do it at all. There is profound discomfort in the creative process, and humans as a rule are not particularly comfortable with ricocheting emotions, which, the Buddhists might say, are another form of *dukkha,* or suffering. The ability to sit with difficult, often contradictory emotions—*I have to write this story; I can't write this story; I must write this story; I shouldn't write this story; they won't like me if I write this story; what will happen if I write this story;*

my grandmother will come back from the dead if I tell this story; nobody will believe me if I write this story; I'll lose my family if I write this story; I have to write this story—does not come naturally to us as a species. But fear is not unique to the individual maker of art: not to you, or to me, or to the writers and creatives who came before us and who will come after us. If we learn to sit with it—to understand that fear, like joy, is simply an expected component of art-making—we will inevitably be graced with the kind of creative fulfillment that comes when we have transcended fear, when we know we have crafted something important and crafted it well. In my workshops, I speak of the *imperative of emotional resilience* in the creative process. When we commit to living a writing life with all of its snares and hazards and landmines, we do so knowing that it is not going to be easy; we can't write anything without fully grokking this and accepting it as part of the process. The discomfort that comes with the process is as much a part of writing as paper is of a book.

Like any kind of anxiety uncontained, fear of the creative process will run roughshod if we let it.

When I am in the throes of writing a new book, I don't sleep well. I often wake before sunrise, my jaw aching with the tension of sleep paralysis. I've long stopped believing I'd remember my dreams in the morning, so now, if I'm jolted awake at 3:23 a.m.—my witching hour for as long as I can remember, when I wake parch-mouthed and panting—I write them down in an illegible scrawl in the small notebook that I keep on my bedside table, even though I'm rarely able to make sense of them at dawn.

It feels as though I dream about my father every night, even though he died suddenly and violently two decades ago. I have told this to no one: I am certain his spirit still walks around, trying to rewind the tape, trying to pause the split second before his car was T-boned by a rusted-out Toyota filled with uninsured teenagers on a hot August Saturday morning in 2002; that I imagine his spirit pacing back and forth on that tree-lined suburban corner in Roslyn, New York, waiting for me to find him, to pick him up, to call the tow truck, to take him home. In my dreams, he is surprised when he realizes what has happened: that he was hit and the ambulances took him to one hospital and my stepmother to another, that he'd spend a week in the Bardo, hovering on the filmy plane between life and death until I removed him from life support and looked at him one last time before they wheeled him away, his mouth gaped open, vacant, in utter shock at what had befallen him, at what I had done, at the fact that he was gone. I believe—I am certain—that he thinks I betrayed him.

Most often, though, my father is in his late fifties when he comes to me, the age he was when I was in high school, he and my mother had divorced, and we spent every weekend together. The dreams are always the same: he glances past me but never directly at me, as though he's looking at something in the distance. I talk to him, reach out to him, beg him to answer; he doesn't respond. I call him on the beige rotary phone that hung on the wall of my childhood kitchen; I hear his voice clearly—*It's Cy Altman, I'm not here right now*—and I leave him a message, but he never calls me back. Or I'm a fly on the wall at a large family gathering of the cousins with whom I no longer speak, and he's in the den with them, having a cocktail. I call his name, but all that comes out of my mouth is a kind of bovine gasp. I see him in the way that Scrooge sees his past in *A Christmas Carol*; my father is a memory, a shadow, clear as a bell, but unable to respond to me.

I wake up panting like my terrier, and believe that he is angry with me because I've written something about us that perhaps I shouldn't have. I imagine that I am dead to him, as I am to many members of my family for writing something that they felt was a betrayal. I didn't toe the party line. I have finally chosen to end the intergenerational cycle of fear and shame, to tell our story of devastation and survival and sustenance, and to shed the shackles of creative suppression.

In choosing to write this story I was not supposed to tell, I have become the ghost, the family apparition that will simply not let our stories rest in peace.

꧁ꦌ꧂

Stories inhabit and possess us. They take over our lives; we cannot shake them. *Stories intervene violently,* writes Arundhati Roy. We must give them attention; we must give them air and water and light, like a garden. They must be respected, allowed to live, allowed to blossom, even if—especially if—we are haunted by them. In *Body Work*, Melissa Febos wrote, *There is no pain in my life that has not been given value by the alchemy of creative attention.*

Those of us who must write usually come to it early, even in childhood. When I was a child, I was a stutterer. As an adult, I told no one. I had been silent about it until I was asked by an interviewer on National Public Radio: *When and why did you start writing? How did it happen for you?*

An uncomfortably long pause: to implicate myself as a stutterer would bring shame to my family, whose children historically speak very early and in full and complete sentences.

I was a stutterer, I told the interviewer.

They went silent.

(No interviewer ever wants to learn, during an on-air interview, that their guest is, or was, a stutterer.)

—so the only way I could finish a thought, I added, *was to write it down.*

I grew up in a loud, pugnacious household in the seventies, the only child of two people who, at worst, loathed each other, and at best, tolerated each other. I couldn't get a word in edgewise. Both of my parents were beautiful, highly creative people whose artistic callings went unfulfilled. My father, a World War II night fighter pilot, a brilliant advertising man and failed poet who carried in his heart the sorrow of creative disappointment throughout his life, and my mother, a musical performer, model, and television singer who gave up the only career she'd ever loved when she married my father and gave birth to me, nine months to the day from their wedding.

Do you know what I gave up for you? she says to me even now when she is enraged, heading into her eighty-ninth year. *Who do you think you are?*

Even now, after four books, countless articles and essays, I cannot answer my mother's questions in complete sentences; the words fall out as a hiccup, a blip, a disconnect. A stutter.

But I know what she gave up. I know what haunts *her* creatively: it was the possibility of making musical art. The chance to fulfill her only creative dream. Her life's regret; she made a choice. A baby, or her art. She chose to become a mother.

When my grandmother walked out on my father and aunt in 1926, she too made a creative choice, and another one when she returned. As I search for the jigsaw puzzle pieces that fit in, trying to understand why she left—these are core parts of the story—I land *here*: my grandmother had been a concert pianist at fourteen and was separated from her music when she married, four years later. She had her children five years apart, my aunt in 1918 and my father in 1923, and she fell into the deep postpartum chemical depression that afflicts most of the new mothers in our family, across the generations. Depression and the inability to fulfill her musical life likely resulted in psychic and emotional isolation, and she fled. When she returned at the height of the Depression—my grandfather held down two jobs and still didn't have two nickels to rub together—a walnut baby grand Knabe piano was waiting for her in the living room of their Brooklyn apartment. Sitting next to her in the back seat of my parents' Oldsmobile in the mid-seventies during a Sunday drive, I watched as her eyes closed and she began to doze off with both hands resting in her lap, moving back and forth—her right hand stretched wide and her thumb rested on an invisible middle C. As a young musician, I recognized the chord structure and the rhythm; she played the ghost of her beloved Chopin's piano concerto in her sleep until the car came to a stop and she was jolted awake.

My mother and my paternal grandmother had no love for each other, but this is part of the story, and what bound and connected them: they both gave up music to raise children. I believe—this is conjecture; I will never know for sure—that my grandmother abandoned her family for creative survival and the visceral desire to make music the way she needed air and water. Conversely, my mother gave up her creative life to have a family, and it has haunted her every day since she married my father in 1962.

I believe the two of them regretted their decisions for the rest of their lives.

❧

My parents both struggled with untreated, complex trauma: My father had been abandoned. My mother lives to this day with physiological dissociation, a kind of congenital analgesia; she didn't know that she was pregnant with me for six months. Together, they yelled, they loved, they laughed, they fought. They lived bifurcated lives of rage and joy and the depleting exhaustion that follows, and I was a witness to their hours, like wallpaper. I began to stutter when I was very young; I couldn't get a word in edgewise in what passed in their minds for civil discussion, and if I did, I was chronically interrupted midsentence: they corrected me, talked over me, got up and poured themselves more chianti just as I was about to get to the good part of the story I was telling them. They flipped the channels on the television set while I was trying to speak, as though I were invisible. Instead of demanding to be heard—throwing a temper tantrum or being otherwise destructive—I stopped finishing my own sentences. I learned instead to quietly watch and listen, and turned from speaking words to writing them. If I was ever going to express myself with words, I couldn't do anything else *but* write.

Some children in the same position would be driven to paint, or draw, or bury themselves in learning how to play a musical instrument. My teenage neighbor Meredith in the next apartment, with whom I shared a bedroom wall, grew up in a restrictive religious household; her mother was a Holocaust survivor who had met her husband in Israel in 1968; they had both been in a displaced person's camp in Germany after the war. Meredith grew up understanding that there were certain things that she was not allowed to say, to ask, to wonder about. Instead of writing about living with two parents who witnessed unspeakable horrors and what that meant for her, she asked her mother for a set of acrylic paints and a few paintbrushes and painted an entire floor-to-ceiling mystical universe of flowers and plants and toadstools on her bedroom wall, not unlike a scene out of *Alice in Wonderland*. Meredith could not speak her truth, but she could paint it, and she did. Years later, she became a professional artist.

Paper is more patient than man, wrote Anne Frank from her attic in Amsterdam before she was sent to Bergen-Belsen. At eleven, I read that sentence—I was still stuttering at eleven—and found it to be wholly true. I couldn't speak without interruption and without stuttering, so I wrote, and I believed that my ability to express myself in this manner could never be taken away from me. No one could cut me off; no one would laugh at my attempting to tell a story about something I'd seen, or heard, or longed for if it was relegated to the page. No one would get up and walk away. No one would ever tell me that the stories I was writing were made up, figments of a bored child's overactive imagination. Writing gave—and gives—me ownership not only of what I see around me, but of the words themselves that I use to express myself fully.

Words allow the stories that haunt us to move through the scrim of imagination and into a place of breath and life.

After my exile from my family, every part of my life began to disintegrate. It was so unexpected, so completely surprising and shocking, that I spun like a top. I obsessed over the loss of people for whom I had a profound affection, and who I assumed had been truthful in their lifelong affection for me. I wrote letters— long, overwrought letters—begging for forgiveness. I wanted my old life back. My health began to collapse; I fell into a suicidal depression; my use of alcohol as a crutch to get me to sleep every night nearly killed me. *What had I done?* I had made what Mark Doty calls an *inquiry into memory. The past is not static, or ever truly complete,* he writes in his essay "Return to Sender," a piece about the intersection of betrayal and memory. *As we age we see [the past] from new positions, shifting angles.* When I wrote my book and revealed the truth about my grandmother abandoning my father and how it touched generations long after it happened, I, too, wanted to examine the past's power over me and my father from new positions and points of view, and from shifting angles.

It took years to comprehend the truth: that I had nothing to apologize for. I had revealed a story that had touched me personally and profoundly, and that made me who and what I am. I could not take on the responsibility of the reactions of others.

A decade later, I rededicated myself to the unknotting of a truth that is as vitally a part of my fundamental makeup as my blood type. My family had claimed that I revealed what I did as a way to hurt them, but they could never elucidate why. There is a difference between gratuitous creative revelation (and its twin, revenge) and the revelations that actually drive a story, and without which that story cannot be crafted. If we are to write, or create at all, we must do the very thing that is scariest: we must honor our creative hearts to overcome the greatest challenge that every artist faces, be it societal, cultural, or personal: the words *you are not allowed*.

That said: who are we to borrow the histories of others, alive or dead, whose stories are compelling, touching, devastating, but whose lives *have not* touched our own? What right do we have *to rifle those lives of their flowers*, to mangle a Woolfian phrase, and use them as the core of our own? When we write about those with whom our lives have not intersected but who we simply find interesting, or are in some way compelled by, that is not memoir; that is biography.

We have no right to rifle those lives of their flowers; those are the stories that *do not* belong to us.

When we write memoir, we also don't get to character assassinate people—alive or dead—because it is convenient revenge masquerading as art, even if we feel that they deserve it. It may feel good at the time—take *that*, you bastard—but revenge writing results in flattened, one-dimensional characters, flattened narrative patterns, a deflating of the complexities of story. An important writer I know famously works out her rage at colleagues, former friends, and family members on the page: her work is lyrical and she is well known, so she gets away with it because she is also recognized as being too dangerous to cross.

We write for what we need as humans: meaning, purpose, and truth. There can be no victimhood, or self-pity. I once attended a craft talk that Dorothy Allison was giving, and she summed up her feelings about revenge writing this way: *You want to write revenge? Then you have to write yourself as fucked up and shameful as your other characters are.*

This work is not for the faint of heart; even now, after hundreds of essays and three memoirs, when I find myself knock-kneed and unable to move forward while I'm writing, I gird myself with the works of truth-tellers made famous for their art of revelation: Suzannah Lessard, Joy Harjo, Ocean Vuong, Barry Lopez, Joyce Maynard, Jericho Brown, Dorothy Allison, Ruth Ozeki, Melissa Febos, Patricia Hampl, Kathryn Harrison, Vivian Gornick, Honor Moore. After Gornick's *Fierce Attachments* was published—a brilliant mother-daughter memoir that unfolds through a series of walks in the author's childhood Bronx neighborhood—the author took to her bed when her mother read it. According to Mary Karr, Carolyn See famously collapsed with viral meningitis two hours after finishing the first draft of her memoir *Dreaming*. See claimed it was her brain's way of saying, *You've been looking where you shouldn't.* Suzannah Lessard was sliced out of the Stanford White family—White was her great-grandfather—after she published *The Architect of Desire*, in which she revealed White's unquenchable and flagrant sexual appetite, the sexual abuse that several members of the family endured after White died, the silences kept, the secret pacts made to maintain appearances. Novelist and filmmaker Ruth Ozeki writes in her beautiful short memoir *The Face: A Time Code* about wanting to be good as a child and knowing that being good meant being reserved and private. When Ozeki shows her elderly parents her autobiographical documentary film *Halving the Bones*, she openly questions the reliability of memory and truth. Ozeki's father asks her outright to never make a film about him. She gives her father her word. She also changes her surname—Ozeki is not her real last name—to prevent family embarrassment, but to also remain true to herself as an artist, and to keep writing and creating.

No writer ever writes alone. Every one of us is bolstered by others who have grappled with different versions of the same conundrum: to write the truth, knowing that there will be consequences, or not to.

We don't choose to create; the creative life chooses *us*. Writers are viscerally driven toward truth and clarity; very few of us are willing to spend two years working on a book that has its roots in malevolence and poison. When storytellers move from silence into speech, we make new life and growth possible both for ourselves and our readers. We crack open the hard shell of shame, expose our stories to light and air, allow our work to breathe, and create magic. Whoever we are—published or unpublished writers; painters or musicians or chefs—if we don't heed the call to create, and give ourselves permission, our worlds darken and fade. Our stories are stillborn; our lives thrum along on a dull, monotonous hum. The healing capacity of storytelling becomes stifled. Shame, that familiar state of excruciating self-consciousness, is permission's plasma; it is shame that is weaponized by those who wish to silence people—almost always women—in their midst. Art-making is the antidote to shame: it diffuses it, releases it, casts it to the wind, allows the creator to breathe again, to heal ourselves and others, to move forward in our work and in our world with, if we are lucky, grace and humanity.

When we ask ourselves, *Why am I choosing to do this, to write this story?* we are expressing the innate shame that comes from the generations of family, the teachers, the clergy, the culture who have admonished us for believing we had anything to say.

Who do you think you are to tell this story?

The permission to write—to make art in whatever form it comes—is proprietary. It belongs solely to its maker. I was my grandmother's granddaughter, and her story touched my life directly and impacted it forever.

Still, we must inquire and investigate our role in our stories, and our motivation behind writing them. There are always ethical concerns, and we would be irresponsible if we didn't consider them. But every one of us is touched by the narratives that are embedded in our lives; this is the human condition, as ancient as the seas. The process of storytelling is paramount to species survival—consider the cultural stories depicted on Greek pottery in 400 BCE, in which entire myths are played out pictographically—and to the metabolization of joy and sorrow. This is why stories and our compulsion for telling them exists in the first place: as a way of remembering who we are, where we come from, what we saw, and what we know to be the truth. And that is the right of every artist.

Six months after my book came out, I phoned my aunt, then in her nineties, to wish her a happy Jewish New Year, as tradition requires one does with the oldest member of the family. We hadn't spoken since the publication.

It was very brave of you to call me—she said coldly.

—*but your story was not yours to tell,* she added, taking nearly an hour to explain how I had singlehandedly destroyed our family by revealing a truth that she had spent almost a century concealing, convinced all the while that she had been successful, even as her brother had fed me the story from the time I could understand words.

I loved you, my aunt said to me, at last. And then she hung up. She would never take my calls or speak to me again.

Rejection is a key part of our core history, and as James Baldwin promised, one that I would write about over and over, until it *became clearer and clearer, narrower and larger, more and more precise.* As in Abraham Verghese's *The Covenant of Water,* in which a single family loses a member to drowning in every generation, in my family themes of primal rejection play out repeatedly in the narrative of our lives over the course of a century.

This was the story I was meant to write, and the reason I believe I was placed on this blue marble: to break the chain and free myself and anyone who comes after me from the strictures of shame encapsulating the myth of a mother who abandoned her husband and children almost a century ago. Through my writing about her, she has morphed from a one-dimensional, tiny, Sabbath-keeping demon to a perfectly imperfect human—a woman stuck in the Bardo between the old world and the new, grasping for some semblance of power and self-knowledge, and utterly devoted to the music that might have saved her.

In writing it, this is what I learned, and what *every* writer learns when they honor the need to tell their story: when we move from the silent to the spoken, we shed light on and create life where there was darkness and shame.

Still, the most difficult decision that any memoirist faces is whether or not our own kernel of truth is important enough to the story to honor and share: Without that kernel, a memoir has no soul. And with it, we risk everything.

5

THE QUESTION OF RISK

*Risk might be our greatest ally. To live
a truly creative life, we always need to
cast a critical look at where we presently
are, attempting always to discern where
we have become stagnant and where
new beginning might be ripening.*

—JOHN O'DONOHUE

IT COMES in so many forms, and it touches our lives daily.

Absolutely everything we do is fraught with risk. The clothes we wear. The food we cook. The way we pray. The people we choose to partner with; telling people that we love them, or telling them that we don't. Having children; not having children. The geographical moves we make. Sleeping with the boss. Sleeping with the enemy. The jobs taken, and the jobs quit. Voicing an opinion, popular or not. Choosing to remain silent. Standing up for what we believe is right, even when it is an unpopular opinion or flies in the face of trend. Writing the thing that is obsessing us, that includes, perhaps, a story about the highly questionable behavior of someone beloved and widely respected, now long dead. Writing about our own questionable, utterly neurotic behavior.

Years ago, I was teaching a memoir workshop that included among my students a National Book Award–winning author of fiction who was starting to write memoir. This person was a brilliant author, and every exercise I presented to the workshop resulted in their writing short pieces that were breathtaking in texture, sound, rhythm. When the workshop was over, eight weeks later, I asked this writer whether they were going to move forward with their memoir as they had imagined it at the beginning of our class, or if it had changed.

Oh, I can't possibly move forward, they answered.

I was stunned. *Why not?*

Because it's too much of a risk, they said, adding that many members of their family would be devastated if the book was ever published.

The family members of concern had been dead for almost two hundred years.

Risk means different things to different people.

Uniformly, though, it means this: *something may be lost because of our actions.*

We may lose face, we may lose family. We may lose work, we may lose friends. We may lose health or money; we may shock those we love. We may be canceled. When Mr. Tanner, the operatic dry cleaner in the late artist Harry Chapin's tragic song, makes his town hall debut and receives a review that concludes, *Full time consideration of another endeavor might be in order,* he has risked it all. The result? Failure.

In January 2023, I spent two weeks at a writers' residency in Maine. There was a lovely kitchen in my living space, and for the most part, I cooked dinner for myself every night. It was bitterly cold outside, but I slept with the curtains pulled back and woke every morning with the winter sun; no matter the temperature, I stepped out each day onto the beautiful, frozen deck that overlooked Rockport Harbor, which I could see clearly because the trees that normally blocked the view had dropped their leaves months earlier. My schedule was mostly the same: sleep, wake, coffee, work, walk, work, sleep. The hours one spends in residency are routine, and are meant to be by design; they are about time, and work, and quiet productivity.

On the night of my arrival, after a seven-hour solo wintry drive from my home in Connecticut, I took myself out for dinner at one of my favorite restaurants, where the chef is a good friend, and I sat at the bar. My phone began to vibrate; I assumed it was my mother or my wife. It was neither: it was Prince Harry, Duke of Sussex.

While I was minding my business and having dinner, no fewer than twenty news posts had streamed into my email, all of them about the breaking reports that a copy of the prince's tell-all memoir had been leaked to a bloodthirsty press. I cared far more than I want to admit even now, but not because of a fixation on The Royals; I cared because of the role of calculated risk in the writing and publication of the book and the inevitable fallout, both of which are universal in the act of memoir and storytelling, even—as evidenced by my grandmother's story—when some of the parties are long gone.

Once you get beyond the weird, gossipy royal angle, the story is your basic, familiar commoner's tale, straight out of Arthur Miller and Shakespeare: the younger, arguably ne'er-do-well son of an important family, after a life of rambunctious, bad-boy behavior, settles down and marries the love of his life who wants nothing to do with her new husband's relations. He's forced to make a decision—it's them or her—and he chooses love, is excommunicated from the family, and spends the rest of his days simultaneously renouncing his place at the table and trying to psychically organize what it means to be disconnected from his clan of origin. No more Christmases, no more Easters, no more family suppers. In his grief, he turns to storytelling—maybe he's a painter, or a composer, or a writer—to share his saga and taxonomize his life experiences. He obsesses over it, perseverates, chews on it like a ruminant, cannot possibly let it go. Because so long as the story exists as told by the young man, his connection to the family—be it bad or good—will *also* still exist. This is where magical thinking comes in: a memoir is written about a notoriously private family by one of its most visible members, and despite revealing the truth—which no one is happy about—the writer believes, somehow, that all will be forgiven.

Every one of us who walks upright has the right to tell our own story the way *we wish it to be known*. Every one of us is responsible for our own narratives, both interior and exterior. And every one of us who tells our own story the way we wish it to be known must *also* be able to live with the fallout—benign or extreme—because, whether we are royalty or a lowly author and teacher of memoir like me, there *will* be fallout, and we cannot predict or control what it will be. This is part of the risk, and when we write memoir, we stare this risk squarely in the face. Fallout is a growling tiger in a cage: unavoidable, and as much a part of the process of writing memoir as cold is to snow.

Magical thinking: if we reveal something that undoes the reputation of one of the parties in the book, we also do *not* then get to play victim and simultaneously plead love and the naive desire to have everything go back to the way it once was. Because it won't be. Ever again.

It took me a decade to fully comprehend this fact: that it is *always* dangerous to write about other people, even in what we think are the kindest of ways, and even if we're telling our own story and not theirs.

The making of art carries the weight of profound risk, and it is the choice of the art-maker alone whether it is worth it, or not.

What is your tolerance for risk? I was once asked by a financial professional, back when I was working in a corporate editorial job. *Could you stand it if the bottom dropped out? Would your value and worth be protected? What will you do if you lose everything? Is it safer to do nothing?*

At the time, this conversation was a source of great amusement; I was living in New York City on a salary of $30,000 a year. The idea that I could save even a dime of it was absurd. But the question of risk stayed with me.

What is your tolerance for risk?

I ask my students this question whenever they want to know whether they *should* or they *shouldn't*: Should they write it, this thing that has become like an albatross in their lives, or should they not? Should they risk it, or should they not? Sometimes, the question is not should they, but *can they? Can they do it? Can they not do it? What will happen if they do? What are the possibilities?* Nothing could happen, and anything could happen. Your work might be met with crickets—silence—or approval or fury. And going in, it's hard to predict (unless we have libeled or defamed someone, and that's another story entirely).

But all of this presumes publication. What we write may be seen by the public, or it may never be.

Beyond the lack of predictability, another problem with risk early on in the process is the creative paralysis that it engenders. The concept of risk assumes a preexisting audience, a book contract, scores of readers drooling and slobbering and climbing over each other to get to your gorgeously bound book, hot off the press, just reviewed brilliantly by the *New York Times Book Review*, which, on its front page, has revealed in the first paragraph a horrible hidden family secret that will kill your mother with shame. If, however, you are just beginning to write, to craft and form the memoir that will bring order to the chaos of your story, you are likely not yet at the book contract stage. I mean: you might be, and if you are, terrific. But if you're not, you're putting the horse before the cart with the sort of creative narcissism and ego that afflicts every single one of us, and that results in our seeing in our mind's eye a finished book long before the first words are even written.

As Lewis Hyde writes in *The Gift*, *Premature evaluation cuts off the flow . . . In the beginning we have no choice but to accept what has come to us, hoping that the cinders some forest spirit saw fit to bestow may turn to gold when we have carried them back to the hearth.* He goes on to quote Allen Ginsberg: *It means abandoning being a poet, abandoning your careerism . . . You really have to make a resolution just to write for yourself . . . in the sense of not writing to impress yourself, but just writing what your self is saying.*

So: craft the book first. Give it time, space, attention. When you have completed it, only *then* can you step into a place where you evaluate: What am I risking by telling this story? What is my intention? My motivation? And only you will know the answers to those questions.

During that final phone conversation with my aunt, I remained silent while she explained to me in minute detail how I had destroyed our family by revealing the story she had desperately wanted to keep secret. She didn't know that her brother had begun telling me the story of their abandonment when I was three years old. She had no idea that he was using me as a sounding board, a repository for the grief he had carried since he himself was a child. She had no idea that, for most of my young life, the story had created such a profound fear of abandonment in me that even the act of going away to camp for two weeks when I was eight upended my life with quiet hysteria and vivid night-mares involving Victorian orphanages and panhandling in rags like one of Fagin's street urchins in *Oliver Twist*.

My aunt did not know that I had grown up in a state that Marianne Hirsch termed *postmemory*; Hirsch, the author of *The Generation of Postmemory*, describes it as the relationship that the generation after *bears to the personal, collective, and cultural trauma of those who came before—to experiences* they *'remember' only by means of the stories, images, and behaviors among which they grew up.* My father's story had *become* my story. I had been touched by it directly, even though it had happened almost forty years before I was born. There was no possible way I could *not* write about it.

In fact, I had not destroyed our family; I had done something far more treacherous. I had taken away my aunt's car keys. I had snipped her brake line. In one paragraph, I had unraveled her tightly controlled family narrative in which everything was perfect, and beautiful, and wonderful. In my search for clarity, for the truth, for patterns of meaning, I had brought dishonor to our tribe and plunged us into the kind of shame born of self-loathing and unresolved trauma. If we had been in another country, I might have been stoned to death; instead, I was given the ancient, devastating punishment of isolation and ostracism and, like the Azazel—the scapegoat—in Leviticus, left to wander the proverbial desert alone for all eternity. In "What You're Saying When You Give Someone the Silent Treatment," a 2021 essay in the *Atlantic*, journalist Daryl Austin describes social and familial banishment as insidious *because it might force the victim to reconcile with the perpetrator in an effort to end the behavior, even if the victim doesn't know why they're apologizing.* Having been disowned by my tribe for telling our grandmother's century-old story, I begged forgiveness for telling a secret that I didn't know was a secret; the apology remains unacknowledged and the silence, deafening. This is storytelling-as-quicksand. I grieved their loss; I still do.

Was writing the few lines about my grandmother and revealing the depths of her humanity and her divided self worth the risk of losing my family, and then *actually* losing them? Had I known that the unthinkable would happen, would I have written it anyway? This is the question that risk poses to every story-teller, every art-maker, every teller-of-truth.

In poet Mark Doty's essay, "Return to Sender," Doty writes at the crossroads of time, memory, and betrayal. In writing about his mother, he says,

When I go to describe the forces that shaped my mother as a girl, I am working from a combination of memory, intuition, evidence, family story; I can make reasonable interpretations and educated guesses . . . . My picturing will distort its subject . . . . This particular form of distortion—the inevitable rewriting of those we love we do in the mere act of describing them—is the betrayal built into memoir, into the telling of memories. But the alternative, of course, is worse: are we willing to lose the past, to allow it to be erased, because it can only be partially known?

Are we willing to erase history and the people attached to it, and pretend that both it and they never happened, rather than allow art-makers to betray the memory of the dead?

In the essay, Doty has sent *Firebird*, the memoir of his childhood, to his father and sister. The latter responds with positive words of support. Doty's father, with whom he has always had a complicated relationship, doesn't respond at all. When the poet writes to him a little while later, the letter comes back to him stamped with the words *Refused, return to sender.*

A memoirist's nightmare is, as Doty writes, *that we will lose people in our lives by writing about them. I have replaced an inauthentic relationship—the conversation we had before, with its many elisions—with an authentic silence. Is that better?*

I do not know the answer to this question, but I do know this: *inauthentic relationships based on conditional love* are as much a betrayal as the compassionate revelations that destroy them. Inauthentic relationships are fueled by risk; nothing is sure, or certain, not even love.

Doty will never know why his father stopped speaking to him. He guesses. Was it that he told the family secrets: His mother's death from alcoholism? His father's embarrassment over the fact that Doty had revealed the number of times that the family moved, suggesting that his father had employment problems?

Doty goes on about betrayal, perceived or not, committed by the artist: *This 'betrayal' is life-giving .... which requires emotional honesty with one's self .... The alternative is silence, a frozen politeness, a fake life.*

In weighing risk, the answer is always subjective. We have no crystal ball. We will never know what will happen. Even if we think we know how people will respond, we can never truly predict it.

⁂

Twenty years ago, an on-air television journalist friend called to tell me that she was putting together a collection of essays and short stories that she'd written over her years in the news business. I thought nothing of it. A year later, her book arrived. In it was a short story that was simply a cut-and-paste of an hour-long text session that she and I had after my father died. In it, I had recounted all of it: my depression, my withering grief, my sadness at how I had been treated by some family members after my father's death, my uncertainty surrounding what my relationship with them would look like going forward, my conjecture about whether my relationship with them had always been inauthentic and conditional on my father's life. And the loss of one of the people I loved most in the world.

I had not yet been able to write about any of it myself.

So I was not at all happy when my friend's book arrived; I was shocked. The wind had been knocked out of me. Yet there was nothing in it that was damning. It was just our conversation, word for word, with no context.

As a journalist, she should have known better: we do not get to borrow conversations verbatim and reprint them between the pages of a book and then claim rights to them. There are copyright issues (which, if I were another person, I would have held her to). I was furious, and when I called her to express my anger, I wanted to know: why had she done it?

Because it was just a good story, she said, weeping with apology. But I couldn't get beyond what I believed to be a betrayal.

My story had not bumped up against hers at all; it had nothing to do with her and had no connection to her in any way beyond the fact that she was on the other end of the text. There had been no emotional excavation on her part, no attempt to apply to her own life what had happened in mine, no context or contemplation. It was simply the reprint of my story, devoid of any perspective.

Risk was never a consideration here. She had never even

thought about it. And when we write anything that involves others, we must consider it; this is called moral tension. Writing about others *must* have its roots in the search for truth and clarity, and that search needs to be made—even when there is enmity between the narrator and her characters—with empathy.

When it comes to risk, I tell my students this: that we must get to a place of internal understanding and acceptance that what manifests on the page *cannot* be undone. In the case of writing from a place of anger or rage, even when it is subtextual, rage is hot; rage is palpable. Rage has its own pulse and rhythm, its own cadence and smell. Rage has its own energy. When we write about something or someone from a place of rage, we will risk—intentionally or not—poking the bear with a spear, be we Prince Harry or a middle-aged writer from Queens. And when we write from a place of confusion—when we grapple to make sense of the patterns of our lives—we will still risk poking the bear.

How do we cope with risk so that it doesn't immobilize us and keep us from creating? We have to understand our motivations and do a searching inventory for the reasons behind *why* we're writing in the first place. Having done that, we have to infer what the responses might be. If we are writing something that includes, say, our college roommate who we discovered slept with our ex, we don't get to assume that the passage of time will diffuse the anger; what is in the past for you is not necessarily in the past for someone else. The best thing we can do: talk to them and let them know that we're writing something that involves them. If they say no, then bear in mind the issues of ownership. Make the decision: is it worth it, or is it not?

On that freezing January night, after I left the restaurant where I'd had dinner and made it back to my Maine residency over-looking icy Rockport Harbor, I gave in and watched Anderson Cooper's interview with Prince Harry. I did not see a celebrity whose goal—whose *intent*—was to throw his family under a bus. His body language, face, and eyes all pointed to this: un-resolved, profound grief born of unspeakable, violent loss and a decades-long obsession with that loss—a nonstop rumination—and the knowledge that he was brought into this world as an extra, a supplement, a *just in case*. His grief was literally *unspeakable*, in that his face and his countenance were in direct contrast to the words coming out of his mouth; they told two very dif-ferent stories—one, what the public knows, and the other, what broke his heart so many years ago when he was a little boy: the loss of his mother. In the telling of his story, he torched every royal rule set down since William the Conqueror. He blew the lid off The Corporation. He knew, going in, that he would risk losing his world, and that is exactly what happened.

Who among us could carry such knowledge of our own ex-pendability in our corpuscles, which is where the dire need to tell one's story always begins, whether one is royalty or not. After Harry's story was published, the world gawked and his family cringed. Sorrow is the great leveler, and it would do well for ev-ery one of us who ever hoped to write or otherwise create our way to meaning and clarity out of chaos to remember that.

Everything we write will touch someone, somewhere, in a way that we have not intended.

Risks, too, are sometimes calculated.

6

TENSION AND SILENCE

*Shame never has a loud clang. The worst
part of shame is how silent it is.*

—VICTORIA CHANG

IN THE early nineties, when my first relationship with a woman ended—we were together for four years despite my still being in the closet; shame kept it a secret from her family and mine—I moved out of our apartment and into my father's childhood Brooklyn two-bedroom with my things: boxes of books, cookware, clothes, guitars, and two cats.

The day I moved in, my father met me there after work and gave me the rundown: *don't turn on the oven; open all the east-facing bedroom windows during the summer to catch the breezes off Coney Island; don't throw anything explosive down the trash compactor; don't use your blow dryer and the microwave at the same time because the apartment runs on two fuses and you'll short out the entire building.* He handed me the keys, deposited a large bottle of Bombay Sapphire gin on the kitchen counter, and took me out for dinner to a local Chinese restaurant, where I drank several large ice-cold vodkas in a row. After dinner, I went back to the apartment I'd spent every Sunday of my childhood in, tried to unpack, and couldn't.

My grandmother had been dead for over a year.

I always thought that she might come home, my father told me.

It had been sixty-five years since she left her family, sixty-one since she returned, and the fact of her abandonment still touched every part of her family's lives, even though it had been buried by a combination of design and shame and become a dead language spoken only by my father, and only to me.

A culture of silence takes years, perhaps, to break, writes Kerri Ní Dochartaigh in *Thin Places*. She is referring to the Troubles, and indirectly to the IRA propaganda poster warning potential informers, *Whatever you say, say nothing.* Seamus Heaney refers to the culture of silence in his 1975 poem about *the tight gag of place.* Victoria Chang, in *Dear Memory*, writes a letter to Silence: *I think I am circling around you, Silence,* she says, *your center, and the closer I get, the closer I am to shame, to the language of shame.*

There is a difference between the political and religious cataclysm that resulted in the horrors of the Troubles and the manner in which mundane silences can quietly eviscerate a family with every passing generation. Chang's words hew to the nucleus of the problem: the beating heart of silence is shame, and shame is the plasma that feeds the withholding of permission. Constraints of silence, be they among families or entire cultures, are shibboleths meant to keep their members from bringing down a cloud of dishonor. Flouting these constraints of silence is implied eventual abandonment: *Speak the truth and you will no longer be a member of this tribe. We won't love you anymore.*

Silence is an act, a blood-pact, a profound understanding that something or someone is not to be spoken of, drawn, painted, sung, and even cooked. It can be almost stunningly mundane. A friend of mine who is a talented professional chef fails every time she makes her great-grandmother's roast chicken. When prodded, they tell me that this great-grandmother lived with the disease of alcoholism in the days before Alcoholics Anonymous; she was institutionalized by her husband, treated most likely with electroshock therapy, and returned to her family unable to function. The one Sunday supper she had been known for—a simple roast chicken, made every week after church—fell to her daughter, who could never make it as well as her mother. An aunt tried and failed. The dish disappeared, never to be cooked again; the great-grandmother's recipe card was removed from her box, which had been passed down through the generations. My chef friend tried to recreate it based on her grandmother's description of it and failed—a simple roast chicken is deceptively both easy and complicated to produce well—as though the recipe itself was a ghost, a tether to shame and the dishonor brought to the family.

When my cousin Harris—a brilliant and deeply gifted musician who had been a prodigy as a child—died from suicide, our highly musical family put down our instruments. Every family holiday had been punctuated by someone taking out a guitar, a mandolin, or a fiddle, or sitting down at the piano. But none of us could bear the joy that music had brought to us while Harris was alive, and also the place of sorrow and memory that it can easily touch. I was given Harris's beautiful Gibson A-5 mandolin by his parents and sister, and for almost a decade it sat in its case, its strings snapping under the weight of my survivor's guilt and heartbreak. Every one of us was devastated by his loss; some of us chose to go through grief counseling, and some of us didn't. For years, music was a reminder: it had belonged to him and only him, and someone else daring to play it felt like kicking dirt in the eye of memory and shining a light on his illness and loss. Suicide in ancient Jewish faith is considered a violation of law, often shrouded in scandal and shame, and hidden. In Orthodox and even Conservative Jewish families, those who commit suicide are often not allowed to be buried with Jewish rites and with other members of their tribe, a restriction that is now widely viewed as archaic and cruel.

A decade after I was excised from my family for writing the truth about our grandmother, a family member wrote me a note:

I never want you to write anything that I might be ashamed to have a great-grandchild of mine read. At the time of her writing, her grandchildren were still in single digits; she was planning her unambiguous stranglehold on permission far in advance.

❧

When is it okay to write my story and when is it not? my students ask me.

Anne Lamott is reductionist about it: *If people wanted you to write kindly about them, they should have behaved better.* Does this mean that all writing, *all art-making that involves other people*, smacks of payback or revenge? No; this is an oversimplification. Most writing and art-making *does* involve other people, to one degree or another; how could it not? (Remember the Venn diagram of interdependence.)

Anne's statement is a straightforward, clear answer to a broader, more complex question: what are the moral implications behind writing memoir that overtly involves the lives and situations of other people? If the family charcoal artist is desperate to make a drawing of gorgeous Great Aunt Gertrude who died in 1918 of the flu epidemic, and whose philandering husband lost every penny they had by betting on the horses—perhaps the family was so shamed that they forbade her name from being spoken ever again and buried her likeness in the bottom of a trunk sitting in an attic—is it within the rights of that artist to go ahead and draw whatever they want without fear of blowback? I believe it is. With the passage of time, silence born of shame can travel one of two routes: It can disintegrate, vaporize, and begin to bear the fruit of compassion. *Who was Great Aunt Gertrude? Why did she marry the philandering husband? Why didn't she leave him? Why did my grandmother leave? What drove her to make this choice, what made her come back, and was she hobbled by sorrow for the rest of her life?* Or it can remain saturated in emotional desperation and creative longing.

⁂

I was in my early fifties when I learned that I had a great uncle who no one ever talked about; silence encased him like a chrysalis, and when I pointed him out to my mother in an old photograph I found buried in the bottom of her desk drawer and said, *Who is this?* the color drained from her face. I will call him Peter; he was my grandfather's youngest brother, who died in 1944.

In the war? I asked my mother.

In an asylum, she answered.

She wouldn't, and couldn't, make eye contact with me.

The story changes from person to person: that he was hit in the head with a ball as a child and became a violent, unpredictable sociopath. (This is my mother's understanding; it's not possible, but likely what she had been told by my grandmother.) That he was a syphilitic. (Possible, but also not likely; census records show him being *mentally unwell* as a young child. He very well might have contracted syphilis as an adult and eventually died of it, but it was most likely not the cause of his mental illness, which dated from his being in single digits). A recent search in the New York City Municipal Archives reveals that he died from a hemorrhagic ulcer, but his diagnostic condition was listed as *catatonic schizophrenia*. He had no social security number at the time of his death, a fact that renders him effectively invisible.

I will never know the truth behind Peter's life and death. I do know that my mother's response was indicative of something potentially catastrophic; I didn't push her, and she didn't offer more. The moral conundrum: do I write about the silences swirling around this man who I learned about late in life, and conjecture who he was, exactly what happened to him, and why my mother, who was eleven when he died, responded the way she did. Do I leave it alone until she's gone, and perhaps even after that.

Are all rocks meant to be turned over?

Peter's story is not mine to investigate because, on initial examination, it does not bump up against mine in any way, so far as I know for sure; only further research could tell me. Another moral conundrum: had I not been digging around my mother's desk drawer, the fact of Peter would never have come up, and the century-old silence would have remained, by design, a silence. And yet: in 2021, the City of New York released municipal photographs taken in 1938 of every city domicile and provided users a database enabling searchers to look for photos relating to them or their families. I searched for my mother's childhood home in Williamsburg, Brooklyn, and what came up was a story unto itself. Outside 312 Grand Street—the ground floor was my grandfather's furniture store—stood my grandmother, pushing my three-year-old mother in a stroller while my grandfather, dressed in a pin-striped suit and a fedora, looks on. Sitting on the stoop next to him is Peter.

It is not mine to write about this any further than I am doing here; morally, I have no stand. I do, however, have every right to wonder, and I always will.

Conversely, I have spent fruitless hours trying to locate the history behind the death of my mother's favorite maternal aunt, who I will refer to as M. I barely remember M—she died when I was five years old—but I do know the stories from my mother: that M took her side when my grandmother was physically abusive; that M dressed beautifully and loved well-made clothes; that she was sharp as a tack and had an excellent sense of humor; that she was ill for as long as my mother could remember with a variety of unidentifiable afflictions, and that at three years old, my mother was taken by train to a tuberculosis hospital in upstate New York where she stood at M's window and waved up to her. Confused by her illness and her lengthy absence, my very young mother was gleeful when M waved down to her niece while cradling a pillow swaddled in a sheet. My mother thought that she had a new baby cousin and wanted to know: *Was it a boy or a girl?*

In fact, if M had tuberculosis, she would have likely infected her entire family with whom she was living in close quarters in Brooklyn. M suffered from manic depression—what is now known as bipolar disorder—and the hospital in upstate New York where my mother was taken by train to wave to her from the window was most likely not a tubercular ward but the former mental institution in Wingdale. Her own daughter also lived with bipolar disorder and what her son referred to as *chronic dread*. The last time I saw M was at my fifth birthday party, held at the long-defunct ice cream parlor, Jahn's, in Queens. My father had given me a simple Polaroid camera as a gift; the first photo I took with it was of him, and the second, of M and my grandmother, sitting together in a booth in front of bowls of ice cream. My grandmother points at the photographer—me—while M looks on, dazed and unsure, and suffering from what I recently learned was late-stage frontotemporal dementia.

I want to know the truth: Did M have tuberculosis? Was the hospital where my mother saw her at the window a tuberculosis ward? Or was it, in fact, an asylum, where she likely endured treatment for what was known severe mental illness. This story *is* mine to investigate because depression runs through my mother's family's bloodline like a stream; it has touched every one of us directly, myself included, to a greater or lesser degree. When my mother tells me that it is not possible for her to have what she calls forgetfulness—dementia—because no one in her family ever had it, I want to know the truth.

I have every right to wonder, and, ethically, every right to look.

When is it questionable to write about another person? When you have absolutely no connection to them, to their story, their history; when you libel, catcall, bad-mouth because this person has somehow enraged you; when there is no *apparent* overlap that you have discovered after research—no interdependent center of the Venn diagram—between your lives. Biographers and historians can get away with writing about other people with whom they have no commonality, but instead (perhaps) an academic interest. Memoirists can and will always be compelled by the lives of others with whom they may share nothing but DNA; our attempts at making meaning out of the chaos of human story is the key that fits the memoirist's lock. We may be so obsessed by a particular story that has touched us in some way that we spend hours researching it. But unless a commonality is revealed, that story is not ours to write as memoir, just as it wasn't when my journalist friend published the text conversation between us in full, simply because in it I had told a good story that she found interesting.

I no longer have a relationship with the family member who asked me the question *Who do you think you are to tell this story?* It took a decade for me to understand the ramifications of her question, and its reach: that the permission to write—the permission to make art in whatever form it comes—is *proprietary*, meaning that it belongs to the maker. We are all, every one of us, touched by the silences and stories that are embedded in art; this is the human condition, as ancient as the seas. This is why stories exist: as a way of remembering who we are, where we came from, what we saw and know to be our truth. The heartbreak that might come with revelation is also *a source of compassion and grace,* as Quaker elder Parker Palmer writes in *The Broken-Open Heart.*

The moral question surrounding the making of art, though, belongs only to the art-maker; the question is fluid, a moving target, subject to specific tribal silences, agreements, and compacts. Creatives must search their own hearts if they know they will be stepping into dangerous territory and ask themselves the right questions before they begin: *What is my motivation for writing this? What am I trying to say? What is my intent?*

7

INTENT AND
MOTIVATION

*We turn to stories and pictures and music
because they show us who and what and why
we are, and what our relationship is to life and
death, what is essential, and what, despite the
arbitrariness of falling beams, will not burn.*

—MADELEINE L'ENGLE

WHY DO we write what we write? Paint what we paint? Sing what we sing? Why do the stories we want to tell become the subjects of our own obsessive minds? Why are writers attracted to the illicit, the creatively dangerous, the stories we've been told not to tell? What is our intention when we make art? What motivates us?

In *How to See*, the painter David Salle writes, *Intent is very elastic . . . it can stand for a variety of aims and ambitions. What has a greater impact on style is how an artist stands in relationship to his or her intention . . . How someone holds the brush will determine a lot. Intention does matter, but the impulse guiding the hand often differs.* It is uncommon for a writer embarking on a new project to allow it to take its own breath and inhabit its own shape, although my novelist and poet friends will likely disagree; musicians, however, find themselves in this place all the time, where rhythm and sound and pacing are often steering the ship, and the musician is there to pay close attention to what the art wants to be, and to be a conduit to getting there.

Will this be a takedown, like Mommie Dearest? an acquaintance asked right before my memoir *Motherland* was published.

I was aghast; I hadn't even considered that it might be likened to the no-holds-barred memoir/exposé written by Christina Crawford about growing up in an abusive household with her adoptive screen star mother, Joan Crawford. When the book came out in 1978, it was widely considered sensationalist, hyperbolic, scandalous. My answer to the question was a firm no: my mother and I had and continue to have a difficult relationship even now, but I was writing the memoir to peel the onion and examine what parental obligation truly means, and what it looks like to have to return to a mentally ill parent's side after that parent experiences a cataclysmic accident that renders them helpless. This was my intent going in, but because the book was written while the story was unfolding, I never knew what was lurking around the next corner. Land mines everywhere. The book had to be written with as open a mind and heart as I could possibly muster—a tall order considering that my mother and I were emotionally estranged at the time of her accident. And so my purpose in the writing was not complex: put these two startlingly different, hotheaded women with a long history of enmity together—a hyper-heterosexual glam-queen former television-singer mother and her bookish, taciturn, chubby, lesbian daughter—and make sense of it. Watch them age in tandem. Unravel it; make meaning from it. Craft a story that was (hopefully) well-wrought, authentic, balanced, and fair. And always bear in mind those words of wisdom spoken by Dorothy Allison: *If you're going to write a character as an asshole, you'd better be ready to write yourself the same way.*

When Christina Crawford wrote *Mommie Dearest*, her intent was, perhaps, fluid: a moving target. Was her intent to crack open the heavily shellacked, Hollywood image of the perfect mother to reveal the breathtaking abuse that lay just beneath the surface? Was her intent to write a story of her own resilience and survival in the face of unthinkable cruelty? Was her intent to write a story that would earn her a sizable chunk of money as a form of revenge against Crawford? In her book, *who* was the primary character: the author, or her mother? Likewise, what was Honor Moore's intention when she set out to write a memoir of life with her father, Bishop Paul Moore, in which she would reveal his bisexuality?

Intent is a plan, however well or badly executed, to achieve a goal. Motivation, though, is different. In the words of Tibetan Buddhist scholar and author Thupten Jinpa, what separates intent from motivation is *deliberateness*. He writes, *Motivation is the drive that moves us . . . and that drive can wax and wane.* Intent, however, is deliberate, *the grand gesture of the work*, says Rick Rubin in *The Creative Act*. Intent is your own internal truth about the work you're setting about to do.

Whenever a student tells me that they are working on a piece of difficult writing over which they have struggled—it might be revelatory, it might be salacious, it might have, at its core, anger over an ancient transgression that fundamentally changed the foundation of their lives or the lives of others, it may speak what has been unspeakable—I ask them to consider this and to consider it carefully: *What is your intent? What goal are you trying to achieve?* And then I ask them: *What is motivating you? What is driving you toward that goal?* Most important, I want them to think about *what will happen if the intent changes as the piece unfolds and evolves organically,* thus altering the motivation.

Because it will.

The art-making process requires a particular degree of flexibility that humans do not naturally possess when we begin the process of writing—or creating anything, for that matter—with intent. We get *grabby*. We get *crave-y*. We want to write what we want to write. We sit ourselves down with a plan of action, even if that plan just lives in our heads and hearts: we're going to write *this* story *this* way with the intent to achieve *this* goal. Damn the torpedoes: we are going to tell our truth. So we begin the work at hand, and we work and work—we make the time, we quiet the noise—and if we are lucky enough, the core truth of the story will begin to reveal itself to us; *we have to listen for it very carefully,* as George Saunders says. But this is a universal truth about the art-making process: nothing is going to be freed up to reveal itself unless we drop the reins, let go of the steering-wheel, take our foot off the brake. Unless we *let go of the side of the pool.*

We all know what it's like: as children we hang on to the pool's concrete edge, kicking our feet, practicing putting our head in the water and learning how to breathe. And then, after a time, someone comes along and tells us to *let go.* After much whining and whimpering, we do; we move toward the center of the pool, splashing and spluttering, completely out of control, terrified that we're going to sink to the bottom like a stone. But we don't.

Applied to the creative process, when we let go of the side of the pool, we're heading into the unknown; we're stepping into a place where, perhaps, the writing (or composing, or painting) has taken on a life of its own. Perhaps the narrator's voice has changed from previous drafts; perhaps the composition has shifted from a major to a minor key; perhaps the painter has been moved to paint over what they began a week earlier. This is when the work at hand begins to come alive, to take shape, even if it's a very vague, very strange shape.

This may not happen immediately, or even close to immediately. I was writing the third draft of my second book, *Treyf,* when I came to the realization that the book was not about what I thought it was; I had a deliberate plan for it—an intention—and in the earlier drafts, I had shoehorned it into a shape to comply with that intention. It would not behave; writing it as I had originally intended was like trying to stuff a live octopus into a pillowcase. With every draft, it changed *organically,* as though it was a living, breathing thing that had taken the car keys away from me. By the time I had a finished manuscript, *Treyf* was a very different story—one that was more about my immigrant grandparents than myself, and how every one of us, regardless of our backgrounds or ethnicities, wrestles with issues of assimilation and the grief of relinquishing the old for the new, the ancient for the modern. In the writing, I came to the place—without looking for it—where I finally understood my grandmother's utter obsession with music and what might have been her life's work had she not become a mother, and how my father, as a small child who had been briefly abandoned by her, sought comfort and sanctuary in the Chopin that she played for him alone as her audience in late afternoons before her husband came home from work.

At a certain point during the writing, I had to step back from the manuscript and ask myself: *What is my intention here? What is my motivation? Is it still the same?* It wasn't. It couldn't have been. And what I discovered was that creative intentions and motivations are not only mutable by their very nature: they *must* be. Woe to any creative who believes that the end result of their work is going to be exactly as they intended it to be at the outset, and the getting-there, just as they carefully mapped it out. Art-making is an act of bravery; when we let go of the side of the pool, we release ourselves from the creative preconceptions that hold us and our work back, and give our work permission to change.

8

REVENGE

When you begin a journey of revenge,
start by digging two graves: one for
your enemy, and one for yourself.

—JODI PICOULT

T WELVE YEARS after my father died, I published my first memoir. During the long process of back and forth with my editor, I sent her a version of my manuscript that contained in it a forty page aside about a particular cruelty I experienced during the week following my father's accident. It was an account of how, shortly after the accident, someone to whom I had been very close—my father once told me that if anything happened to him, I should seek wisdom and support from her—was brutally unkind in a manner so stunning that it would have made my father come screaming back from the dead had he been able. Her behavior was so breathtakingly bad that it verged on the comical, proving the point that sorrow and humor share the same DNA. When I described what had happened to me—to us; my father's memory was involved—my therapist pointed me to the famous episode of *Curb Your Enthusiasm* when Larry David comes home to discover that his mother has died but no one let him know because she didn't want anyone to bother him.

Do you laugh, or do you cry?

It took me forty pages of telling the story to get what had happened *exactly right*; the narrative drew its breath from the rhythm of quiet, seething rage and resentment, how they can snowball in the right creative climate and result in mundane tragedy turned upside down. In my narrator's case—my narrator is me, as character—it also resulted in unresolved and complex grief that follows her like the trail of filth that chases Pigpen through life in the *Peanuts* cartoons.

I waited breathlessly for my editor to respond to my

manuscript; when it came back to me, those forty pages over which I had tearfully slaved had been sliced out of the story like a cancer.

Excellent writing, my editor wrote in a margin note. *But absolutely nothing to do with the story.*

I was surprised, upset, and certain that my editor did not grasp what I was trying to say with my brilliant explication of unfairness and appalling callousness at one of the most horrendous moments of my life. She didn't get it. I called her and politely told her so.

Oh, my editor said, *I understand what you're trying to say. But it has absolutely nothing to do with the story.*

With the stroke of a pen: forty pages on the cutting room floor.

At first, I gulped: How dare my precious brilliance be deleted? How dare the words I slaved over be so blithely scrubbed from the manuscript? How dare the editor dither with, I thought, one of the main threads of the narrative?

I explained myself to her again; she said *nope.*

I was infuriated and clung to those forty pages like a drowning man clings to a life preserver.

And then I realized: she was right.

Once I stopped talking and actually started *listening*—this is key when you're blessed to work with a good and thoughtful editor—I realized that I needed to reach a place of creative comprehension: that the painful cruelty I had experienced at the hand of someone I trusted had to be transcended—I had to move beyond it to a place of compassion and some degree of understanding—if I was ever going to write anything else disconnected from our story. My creative attachment to her betrayal had to be snipped like a wire.

When we write, we want to create work that is authentic, pure, reflective of our stories, our lives, our worldviews; we do not want to have to ask permission to create it, or wait for someone to give it to us. Most of us step into the space of creativity with—and I absolutely believe this—the most untainted of motivations; like the prehistory cave artists that Robert Macfarlane speaks of, humans instinctively want to leave evidence of our being present, of our stopping time, of our being *here*. Some creatives want to make art as a way of achieving popular success, and any artist who says they've never dreamt of it is not being truthful; it's human nature to want success and notoriety—to crave it—and one that we must be attuned to vis-à-vis our own expectations and drives. When George Saunders talks about having to get quiet and listen to what the work is trying to tell them he is leaving out the fact that we also have to listen to the *work's* answer to why it is being made—why it *wants* to be made—and whether that answer is one that involves transcendence, or retribution.

As much as we'd like to think otherwise, revenge is a primal and ancient impulse; many of us are taught about it in childhood Judeo-Christian religious education. In Leviticus 24:19–21, the passage states, *Anyone who injures their neighbor is to be injured in the same manner: fracture for fracture, eye for eye, tooth for tooth. The one who has inflicted the injury must suffer the same injury.* A few thousand years later, Jesus turned that idea of vengeance on its head in the Sermon on the Mount, when he preached *turn the other cheek.* And yet: we naturally gravitate to the earlier passage. When we are hurt, we want to hurt back because we are certain that it serves *them* (whoever they are) right, or they will learn from it, or we will somehow vanquish them, embarrass them, humiliate them. My mother's favorite promise for exacting revenge is a violent, bracelet-rattling finger-wave and a simultaneous shriek of *I'll fix you*. Newton's third law makes science of it: *For every action in nature there is an equal and opposite reaction. If object A exerts a force on object B, object B also exerts an equal and opposite force on object A.*

Revenge writing can be widely witnessed on social media: someone posts an opinion about something on their Facebook page, or on their X (formerly Twitter) feed, another person takes offense to it, and thus the battle begins, slowly collapsing under the weight of enmity born from *I'm right and you're wrong*. Roxane Gay says it most directly: *If you clap, I clap back.* Long and arduous creative battles have been fought in the revenge arena: Gore Vidal and William F. Buckley clashed famously (and violently) on television; Ayelet Waldman and Katie Roiphe went toe-to-toe on Twitter; sisters A. S. Byatt and Margaret Drabble clung to their ferocious childhood enmity and dragged it into their work when Byatt wrote *The Game*, a novel about sibling rivalry, and sent a copy to Drabble with a note signed, *With love.* A well-known memoirist spent five years writing obsessively about a former friend and literary colleague after the latter made a simple, private social error for which she apologized profusely. The colleague's wise response? To mourn the demise of the friendship, to walk away, and to let the flakes in the literary snow globe settle.

Anne Lamott's famous words about forgiveness can also be translated to revenge: *Not forgiving is like drinking rat poison and waiting for the rat to die.* Swap out the words *Not forgiving* for *Seeking revenge*.

But when a situation is hot—and it can be fresh or it can be ancient; the question of creative revenge hobbled me in the early days of writing a memoir about my enmeshed, vitriolic relationship with my elderly mother—I try (and often fail) to take the Buddhist approach that I wrote of earlier: I put down my sword, turn my back, and step away from the inclination to get back at my subject for something they've done that's hurt me. I will not write ill of them, I will not libel them, but I *will still* allow myself to write about them, and to (try and) do so fairly.

I have a first reader (my wife) and a second reader (another artist friend), and if they tell me that anything I've written smacks of attempts at vengeance, I know, from a creative standpoint, that the work needs to be recast, just as the chapter in which the forty pages were excised from my first book by my editor needed to be rewritten, and that section, redrafted.

Anything that I have written in a fury—quickly, in an enraged splutter—has to rest before it is shared with anyone, including my wife. It has to settle and breathe before it moves on for other eyes because—my forty pages being the point—sometimes, one just needs to get something out of one's system, with all its hooks and jabs and sucker punches. Those forty pages were completely valid and perhaps even fairly well written, and they belonged nowhere but in my journal.

Human nature: The desire to be right. The desire to be first. The desire to tell the truth about *Something That Happened* as *we see it*, to the exclusion of everyone else around us. The desire to convince those around us who are *wrong wrong wrong* about fill-in-the-blank because we know better. These desires conspire against us where revenge writing is concerned.

I begin every one of my writing workshops with the same question: *Why are you writing the piece you brought here? What is the motivation for wanting to craft your story? What are you hoping to achieve aesthetically and artistically?* Usually, the answers have to do with wanting to attain clarity, or to make art from the human and mundane, or to leave a record. But once, a student workshopping a section of their memoir told me plainly: *I want to write this memoir to exact revenge on someone. Why else would I do it?*

It was not something I expected to hear from him: he was a shy-looking fellow, with warm eyes and an engaging, kind smile. The juxtaposition of desire for reprisal and *nice* was startling and made me nervous, but I appreciated his honesty. I answered him with words about how revenge writing impacts the *craft* of writing (actually, the craft of *anything*; I once knew a middling musician who regularly tried to outdo her talented prodigy sister, and all that resulted were Bach's cello suites played hard and angry and a little sharp, all of their sweetness siphoned out like gasoline from an old car).

Revenge writing—conscious or not—is never, *ever* a good creative intention. Revenge writing deflates language, destroys art, flattens souls, renders characters clichéd and one-dimensional and lifeless. It dilutes human complexity and possibility from the story; it negates human frailty. It slows the pace and pulls the reader into the muck of someone else's poison. There is a difference between the kind of gratuitous revelations that power revenge and the revelations that drive the story forward, without which the story would not exist. If we are certain that telling a story about someone who did something heinous will *get him back because the asshole deserves it*, we also have to ask ourselves: *and then what?* How do we move our characters through their lives? How do we show our narrator moving through their life? How do we move through our lives? *What comes next after revenge?* Will revenge writing give the reader the fullest, clearest sense of who a character is at the human level, be they kind or cruel? No. This is what readers deserve, and what good memoir—good art-making—requires. Revenge writing smacks of desperation, of the writer's back being up against a wall and their coming out swinging; it is a shivering, panting dog that will do anything for a bone; it is out of options. Revenge writing is always a cheap shot.

The desire to retaliate is born of perceived lack of control coupled with the emotional violence of sorrow; it is the creative manifestation of wanting to make the pain stop. In Jane Hirshfield's words, *A wise elder once told me that 'every human heart has in it a hole that can't be filled . . .' We live our entire lives in its company and its dread. And we make our choices because it is for each one of us, there.*

As creatives, we make our choices; all we can do in our imperfect humanity is strive for the right ones.

9

PERFECTION AND COMPARISON

Perfectionism is a mean, frozen form of idealism, while messes are the artist's true friend.

—ANNE LAMOTT

Y EARS AGO, a memoirist friend told me that she begins the writing of every new book in a notebook that she purchases specifically for that occasion. Sometimes, the notebook sits untouched because heaven forbid she make an error on the first page and render the story that she's writing doomed from the start, and the precious notebook, defective. I understand this problem firsthand because I have an entire shelf in my office dedicated to empty, blank journals of every form and shape: Moleskines, fancy leather journals from Italy, little Japanese notebooks, hardback laboratory notebooks I bought at the Harvard Coop in 1983 when I was a junior in college, an outsized German notebook I bought in Tromsö, Norway, four-hundred miles above the Arctic Circle while on a work trip having to do with salmon, where there was such limited light that it threw my circadian rhythm off and I barely wrote at all.

Why don't I write in these blank journals? Because I am afraid to. I'm afraid of making a mistake. Afraid of going down the wrong road. Afraid that I will lose the notebook and have to go back to square one. Afraid that I will be wrong. Just plain *wrong*. Afraid of breaking the rules. Afraid of being a fraud. Afraid of not being as good as my writer friend who just landed a piece in *The New Yorker*. Afraid of not being perfect.

I once heard an author tell a group of new writers that she writes the first forty pages of every book longhand because that early on, no memoir has any right to look completed, by which she means: writing on a computer often makes a manuscript look finished—designed—far earlier than it should, and it tricks the brain into thinking that it is. I understand this: in my workshops, I will often receive memoir excerpts that have been *designed* by the writer—literally *designed*: the font might be purple and a large, round sans serif style made popular by Milton Glaser in the sixties; they might even have sketched out the cover—who has spent hours, days imagining the final book. Very often, these same students forget to put their name on their manuscripts. Very often, they ignore my request for double-spaced, twelve-point, Times Roman type and instead submit their work written in tiny, nine-point, sans serif style, single-spaced, so that they can squeeze ten thousand words onto the requested number of pages, rather than the twenty-five hundred I've asked for. More is not better; it is just more.

Very often, though, these students—like me with my piles of journals—are just *stuck*, and are so *disconnected from*, *afraid of*, *worried about* the craft of the piece they are wanting to write that they'll focus on how it looks rather than sweat over the story and create a first draft that is abysmal, but a first draft nonetheless. Anything else is distraction, hobbled by perfectionism.

Write as if you were dying, wrote Annie Dillard in *The Writing Life*. She did not say *find the most perfect purple font as if you were dying*.

I am a horrible painter; as a child in kindergarten, I came home covered in fingerpaint. I was the kid who always cut the paper snowflake in half.

My cousin Nina is the family painter; she followed in the

footsteps of two of her paternal aunts, who worked in oils and learned how to make lovely still lifes at the Woodstock Art Students League, where they spent their summers in upstate New York.

But as a child, I was always drawing outside the lines in the coloring books my grandmother brought me. My people (and dogs, and cats) were stick figures with gaping eyes and enormous, disproportionate feet; now, in my fifties, they still are. I try, very hard, to make them charming and whimsical and artistically idiosyncratic, like Maira Kalman's characters, but in truth, they're flat and boring, and I cannot bear to look at them.

Some years ago, on one of our late summer trips to Maine, we invited one of my wife's colleagues to join us for a few days with his two young kids. Simon, like Susan, is a book designer, and an incredible illustrator and painter, so early one evening over cocktails and cheese curls, I asked him to teach me how to make some remedial watercolor paintings. I'd brought a little set of paints and some special watercolor paper with me, and together the five of us set ourselves up on the screened-in porch as the sun was just beginning to dip, and Simon gave us a rudimentary lesson.

The kids produced paintings that were kid-like, but Simon proclaimed them *excellent starts*. Susan painted a vibrantly colored landscape, and Simon's little painting was frameable. My painting was disastrous—like Mark Rothko on bad ayahuasca—because I had no sense of how watercolors work: they bleed, they flow, they're completely uncontrollable and unpredictable unless you're either a master or you're comfortable with surprise.

Wow, said Simon, looking at my painting. *That's so interesting—*

That's great for a start, said Susan, looking over my shoulder.

I decided, right then and there, that I'd never pick up a paintbrush again if I couldn't make something that wasn't remotely good. I would never be one of those women who sets up her ancient easel on a bluff over the pounding Atlantic, wearing a straw hat and ChapStick and threadbare khakis.

A few years later, I attended an exhibit at the Yale Center for British Art with Susan and Simon, about field books, those lovely pocket-sized notebooks carried out to gardens and on walks in England during the nineteenth and early twentieth centuries. Often a combination of narrative diary and watercolors painted on the spot, not one of them was perfect. Some of the art was better than others; some of the handwriting was illegible, and some was magnificent. All of the books were evidence of a kind of personal obsession rather than a comparison to the work of other artists. These people were not painters being commissioned to make their art; they were college students, teenagers, mothers and fathers, grandparents, middle-class people who liked to walk, and look, and describe both visually and narratively what they saw.

It was a transforming creative moment for me: I realized how limiting perfectionism can be, that its roots are born in the hierarchy—the good, better, best—of comparison. And that perfectionism touches every part of our creative worlds, always detrimentally.

Five years after Simon and Susan and I painted our watercolors in Maine, I am addicted to painting my shitty little watercolors of my favorite place on Earth. I show them to no one else but my wife, and rarely her. Every weeks-long trip to Maine results in bad watercolors of the exact same landscape filling a little painting notebook. Every palate is the same: husky grays, murky greens and browns, dusty blues.

My cousin Nina loves painting houses and gardens emblematic

of safety and security; I paint watercolors of the crashing ocean and the rocky Maine shore and the broad, gray sky. My paintings (I can hardly call them that) are evidence of a lack of control—my visual story of my father's abandonment and all of the fury that came with it—and expansiveness and recognition of my human diminution in a big, wide world.

There's a reason we are drawn to gazing at the ocean, writes Rick Rubin. *It is said the ocean provides a closer reflection of who we are than any mirror.*

So I paint these bad watercolors for myself alone, and still—I cannot deny it—I measure their progress, as though the possibility of commodification and therefore value is just a breath away. The message that I learned early on, that we all learn: if you can't sell the fruits of your labor, then why bother.

If I paint for myself and only myself, does it count?

If you write for yourself and only yourself, making mistakes, not worried about perfection, are you really writing?

Yes. You are.

⁂

The only thing I can draw that is empirically perfect is a three-dimensional box.

I have been drawing this perfect three-dimensional box since I was nine years old, when Nina—she is also a skilled charcoal artist who studied for a while in Florence—sat me down during a family dinner and said, *May I show you how to draw something?* I loved, and love, her, and she took out a fine black Micron pen and drew a perfect box on a cocktail napkin.

Now you, she said, handing me the pen.

It was like magic; I was astonished.

Perfect! she said, and I was thrilled.

I have been drawing it ever since. I drew it in my school note-books, in my high school looseleaf binder, in my college note-books, on legal pads at my editorial job when I got bored, on bad blind dates, waiting to be selected for jury duty, waiting at the DMV, waiting for an MRI. It's my go-to, my crutch, my security blanket. I paint vast gray endless Maine skies, and I draw boxes, which by their nature keep things neat and tidy and contained, instead of a mess, like my bleeding, uncontrolled, shitty water-colors. Because I was taught: messes are the sign of a confused, distracted, undisciplined mind. Messes are embarrassing, and meant to be hidden. Messes are the sign of a secret mental illness, an unraveling of thought, a psychosocial disorder. One imagines hoarders: the Collyer Brothers.

Nobody likes messes.

It is human nature to strive for perfection; we are born with this glitch the way we're born with opposable thumbs. I want to—I *must*—get the story of my grandmother's leaving absolutely right; only perfection will do her, and us, justice.

But, as essayist Patricia Hampl has written about memoir, it *is a peculiarly open form, inviting broken and incomplete images, half-recollected fragments, all the mass (and mess) of detail. It offers to shape this confusion—and, in shaping, of course, it necessarily creates a work of art, not a legal document. But then, even legal documents are only valiant attempts to consign the truth, the whole truth, and nothing but the truth to paper. Even they remain versions.*

The problem with perfectionism—with the sense that ev-erything that every human produces in whatever form it comes needs to be out-of-the-gate perfect, be it a memoir or a watercolor or a popsicle stick box or a piano concerto—is that it also means that there is no room for skill-building, for learning, for riding a bike with training wheels and experiencing that moment of sheer delight when they're removed. It leaves no place for accomplishment and no sense of the joy that comes with it, whether it's toilet training a toddler or driving a golf ball long and straight or learning how to make a loaf of sourdough bread or crafting an essay or writing a memoir.

Perfection bleeds over into every part of our lives as adults, from work to home to yoga to piano lessons to raising children to the diet culture that hobbles us no matter who we are. Bonnie Friedman, in her great book *Writing Past Dark*, admits to immediately flipping to the back flap of a new book in a bookstore to try and determine the age of its author. *Was it the perfect author with the perfect life and the perfect credentials who landed the book contract? How had she managed it?*

How much time did Bonnie's fretting, comparing, and bemoaning whether her own work was perfect or not take away from the joy and pleasure that comes from the act of creating itself?

For creatives, perfectionism is the devil, making uniform automatons out of humans and pouring flawless, quick-dry concrete over the idiosyncratic stories that separate us from the gods. *If people reach perfection,* wrote T. H. White in *The Once and Future King, they vanish.*

Our humanity certainly does.

The simple truth: joy and pleasure come from the work itself, as the Bhagavad Gita says, and not necessarily a racing toward a perfect end result, which is directly connected to human ego, competition, quantitative value, shame, and fear. *When I am writing,* says Henri Cole in the *Paris Review, there is no pleasure in revealing the facts of my life. Pleasure comes from the art-making impulse, from assembling language into art.*

But:

We are only human.

And perfectionism has very long tentacles, like a squid.

It exists in families like genetic coding, getting passed down like the ugly family heirloom that no one really wants until someone accidentally drops it and it shatters into a million pieces.

The first piece of writing I ever published appeared in a small Nashville newspaper in 1990—a book review about a newly discovered collection of Thomas Wolfe's essays and letters. My father, who was for the most part proud of my accomplishment, suggested that I bring it to a family gathering so that my extended family could see it. My aunt, a former teacher, read it, squinting at the Xerox, and then handed it back to me.

There's a grammatical error in the third paragraph, she said, loud enough for everyone to hear her.

A few nights later, over dinner in my apartment, my father's own creative, competitive monsters took over; he had been a successful advertising executive for forty years by then, but also a failed poet and writer. He longed to write the story of his mother leaving and returning; he had been warned not to, and what he did write emerged strangled, gasping for air. That night, he had a copy of my review next to his plate, read it again, looked up at me, and said, *Well, it's nice, but it's not the* New York Times.

I didn't submit anything for publication for years after that;

permission had been granted by the little Southern newspaper that ran my review. Permission had been revoked by someone I loved, who, I determined, must have been right.

When perfectionism is driving, writes Brené Brown, *shame is always riding shotgun.* And shame, when it emerges—which it always threatens to do when we are creating anything, be it my shitty watercolor paintings or my third memoir—is a destroyer, an ancient Talmudic barometer of the good-or-bad binary. *An evaluation.* Shame attacks us at the heart of who we are as humans; it renders us naked and bare, standing before a judge who will decide whether we are acceptable to the community, or not. And if we are not, that shame will be cast over us—and by extension, our tribe—rendering us paralyzed, devastated, humiliated. *On the outskirts of every agony sits some observant fellow who points,* wrote Virginia Woolf, and this is true. This is shame at work; that observant fellow dissociates himself from it, from the sticky awfulness of it. Shame becomes *them versus us; the bad versus the good.* The acceptable versus the intolerable.

But when we make the decision not to do something at which we are not absolutely, empirically perfect—we decide not to bake the bread, or throw the pot, or write the short story, or sing the song, or write the poem—we're depriving ourselves and others of the *possibility* of beauty. We're depriving our own hearts of the kind of spiritual generosity that only ever comes from making art for the sake of making art. Forget about commodifying the thing we're doing: this isn't about making money. Years ago, a childhood friend's grandfather told his adult kids that they were wasting money on their daughter's dance lessons, even though she was in love with dance and everything about it. She wasn't great at it—a little klutzy—but that didn't matter; it gave her joy. But her grandfather's implication was that she would never be a commercial success at it, so why even bother. Money spent on lessons, in his estimation—he was a man who had lived through the Great Depression and fought in the Pacific during the Second World War—had to equal money earned, otherwise it made no sense. One of the highest hurdles any maker of art has to leap is the (very Western) assumption of quantitative value, the salability of one's artistic work, and its monetization. What we never consider is that the value of artistic work, however bad or good, is in the process itself, rather than the result.

True permission to create demands the promise of art-making without fear of imperfection, evaluation, judgement, or commodified value. When we step into a place of meditative creation—that moment when we sit down at our potter's wheel, or at our desk, and it's nine in the morning and the next time we look up it's three in the afternoon; we have slipped into that flow state where the words seem to come effortlessly, hobbled by neither shame nor fear, nor the voice of an elder saying to give it up because it's not impeccable—we are no longer bound to the stultifying problems inherent in perfectionism. Creative paralysis disappears. Instead, we've become a vessel through which the work travels in a way that can only be described as mystical. Creating without looking over one's shoulder at what everyone is thinking or into the future at potential value results in *agency*.

10

HUMILITY

To learn which questions are unanswerable,
and not to answer them: this skill
is most needful in times of stress and darkness.

—URSULA K. LE GUIN

I HAVE AN entire shelf of notebooks sitting on the old warping white IKEA bookcase sitting perpendicular to my desk in my home office. At last count I had nine, dating back to the mid-seventies, when I was thirteen. The earliest writing in them is loopy—literally *loopy*: round and swirly and written in too-thick purple magic marker—and then eventually I moved on to spluttering blue BIC pens, and at some point, my father gave me an orange fountain pen like the one he had used in grade school in the thirties. That one dripped and exploded everywhere, and eventually I just gave up and decided to write in pencil because pencil is impermanent: it can be erased and smudged in the event that one manages to say something self-condemning, which is inevitable in notebooks.

On another shelf—this is on the bookcase where I keep important volumes of poetry: Gary Snyder, Merwin, Audre Lorde, Marie Howe, Donald Hall and Jane Kenyon, Mary Oliver—I have at least six of them of varying sizes: large, small, very small. There's a leather one that I bought in a little shop on Fourth Street in Berkeley, a rubberized one (this was a mistake), a woolen tartan one given to me by my wife. On the little shelf that sits on my desk behind my computer I have three or four more, including one that is now in tatters and that I used to take notes during my first summer residency at a writers' workshop in Oregon, where there was so much wisdom flowing through the air that I couldn't keep up with it all. When I'm traveling for work, I always take that one with me.

The most important one—my father's childhood three-ring binder, pebbled black leather, given to him by his sister when he was a grade school student—sits on the corner of my desk at all times; I make notes for all of my books in it, in the earliest stages of the process. When the books are published, I clip together the pages from the notebook and store them together with the manuscript. This is neither posterity nor affectation: it just reflects my inquiry into the process—how I got from point A to B, what was going on in my life at the time I was writing, and how it affected my work, my voice, my day-to-day, my hope. The pages are interspersed with marginalia: lists, recipes, music I'm listening to, poetry, clipped-out photos, sections of articles. I have many artist friends who keep the same kind of journal, be they painters, photographers, singer-songwriters, gardeners. Each of them considers the act of notebook-keeping an almost spiritual necessity for their work and their practice, especially if that work has been hobbled by issues of permission; unless we're keeping our journals with the expectation that they will be published—and who among us believes that—the act is one based in humility and grace.

Perhaps this is a fetish understood only by writers and doodlers alike, that we would ascribe such importance to the container for words in a manner that is as essential as the finished work itself. An author friend once told me that the novelist Ruth Ozeki introduced her to the concept of keeping a process journal while she's writing her books. I was mystified. If one is a creative, then aren't *all* notebooks process journals? Isn't this why some of us are as compelled by the journals of everyone from Virginia Woolf and Da Vinci to Anne Truitt and Annie Dillard as we are by their actual art? Notebooks contain the stories behind the stories, *even* when they hold not a shred of evidence to be found in the final result. Notebooks are the viscera and the DNA of art-making; they are proof of life and human frailty behind our dodgy attempts at perfection, which is as tightly linked to problems of ego and humility as it is to external oppression and shame.

Notebooks are where we first learn to give ourselves permission to create.

Notebooks and journals *are* different: I often use the words interchangeably, and that is my error. I think of notebooks as those places where anything goes, beginning in grade school where we wrote notes on the back pages to the kid sitting next to us, or where we might copy down stray bits of poetry we love, or a rewrite of a paragraph, but in a different tense. Journals, as I've always understood it, are meant to be written in daily—the *jour* in journal comes from the French for *day*. They are separate, more secretive. I probably wouldn't care too much if you found my notebooks upon my death, but my journals? They are going up in flames with me. The most familiar journal contains a boundary between *mine* and *yours*: it is the lock-and-key version a lot of us remember from childhood. Mine was cream leather, painted in gold along its edges with what publishers call a *top-stain*. It had been gifted to me with great fanfare by my father on my seventh birthday, after I expressed concern that the very first notebook he'd given me—that brown merle one with the black-taped binding in which I decided to write the story of my life when I was three—was *not so secure*; unless I hid it, my parents, grandmother, aunt, and uncle, might be able to read it. It is at the age of seven that most of us begin to comprehend that some of our stories are not meant for public consumption and that we need a secure place to put down our thoughts that is ours and only ours. Which is why, when I came home from first grade one day and found that the little cloth loop feeding into the tiny padlock on my diary had been cleanly snipped with pinking shears, I became woozy with shame and embarrassment; whoever had done the snipping now knew my innermost thoughts, which had mostly to do with the earliest indications of a visceral and primal sadness, an otherness, and a prepubescent crush on, in equal measure, David Cassidy and Olivia Newton-John. I'm sure that the handwriting was impossible to read. This didn't matter. I thought I would explode with horror.

The fear of being found out—of having someone know my private thoughts; had I given *them* permission?—was tinged with shame, so I confronted no one, and no one ever admitted to the snipping. Although the only person in the house with pinking shears was my maternal grandmother, I maintain that it was not she who did the snooping; she was enormously respectful of my privacy, even when I was a child. Plus, I would learn years later that she had her own secrets to carry: she was a lesbian involved in a sixty-year relationship with a woman who lived in Greenwich Village, and was otherwise in a loveless marriage with my grandfather (who was carrying on a long affair with a local Brooklyn nun), and so she naturally understood the concept of discretion.

After I made the discovery that someone had broken into and read my diary, I ripped out the few written pages and tore them into pieces, put the book in my desk drawer, and never saw it again; it disappeared, along with the furniture, when my mother moved into Manhattan, postdivorce, ten years later. This didn't mean that my mother has not had access to my private writings since the demise of my little lock-and-key diary: I came home from college to her Manhattan apartment and inadvertently left a few of my notebooks high up on a shelf in a closet in the den, where I slept for two years after graduation. What compelled me to do this I do not know, but they lived there, long forgotten until a few months ago, when I found them sitting on the den nightstand; my mother had discovered them one day and was using them to write random notes, tearing out pages when she needed something blank on which to write a phone number or a shopping list. I was outraged, and when she came into the den and I said, *You're using my notebooks as scratch pads,* she answered, *Yes—what do you want for dinner?*

I began keeping a notebook in earnest when I was in my later teens because I wanted to understand what was going on in my life, no matter how mundane it was; I needed to do this for myself, and not for anyone else. At the time, my life was imploding: my parents were divorcing, I was discovering that I preferred girls to boys, I was trying to understand who I was and what I was going to become. I maintain this is, at core, why any of us keeps a notebook, and that it has little to do with creative arrogance or the assumption that someday it will be turned into a book. Joan Didion, in her essay "On Keeping a Notebook," says, *I write entirely to find out what I'm thinking, what I'm looking at, what I see and what it means, what I want and what I fear.* In other words, to write privately as a reflection of one's interiority, to bear witness to one's mind, unaffected by demands and requirements of external trend and cultural style.

Madeleine L'Engle takes this further:

I have advice for people who want to write. I don't care whether they're 5 or 500. There are three things that are important: First, if you want to write, you need to keep an honest, unpublishable journal

*that nobody reads, nobody but you. Where you just put down what
you think about life, what you think about things, what you think is
fair and what you think is unfair.*

(L'Engle's *The Crosswicks Journals*—her series of memoirs
written at the intersection of family, faith, and art—might have
started out life as her private notebooks; we don't know this for
sure.)

More than anything else, notebooks and journals are repos-
itories of safety and sanction, places where we allow ourselves
with humility to stumble and fall, to love and long for, to look at
things we're told either don't exist or never happened, to unravel
and make sense of them.

* * *

As an only child, I did not have the ability to share my thoughts
about what I was surrounded by with anyone; I recognized my
mother as not being safe to share with because her response to
difficult conversations was to trivialize them. My father was more
inclined to share whatever I told him with his sister and extended
family because they were sources of wisdom and perspective for
him, but when things in my life that were troubling came back to
me over formal family meals, I was mortified and felt betrayed,
and then I made mental notes of it: some things are not meant to
be shared—sometimes not even with people you love.

In my teens, my notebooks evolved from my loopy magic-
markered writing dotted with little hearts and daisies and peace
signs to short paragraphs about things that I was beginning to
face but could not share anywhere else: my mother's Scotch-
drunk boyfriend driving us at night on winding upstate New
York country roads in his Volvo to get from a party to the motel
we were all staying in, nearly killing us; the realization that

my grandmother was a lesbian; the awareness that my mother likely had an affair with my father's best friend, a pillar of the community and the same man made to leave town under threat of incarceration for his affection for little girls, myself included; my best friend's and my own dog dying on the same day; the discovery that my childhood terror of a particular, widely beloved family member was, in fact, with merit; my first drink; my first weed; my first sex; my joyful, petrifying discovery that I preferred women; falling in love with someone who did not love me back; falling in love with someone who did; the acknowledgement that I was an outsider in my own family, and the confirmation of it thirty years later, with my excision. All these realizations and firsts have eventually made their way into my books and essays, and I have gone so far as to use my 1979 diary to corroborate my mother's absurd threat of suicide when I refused to let her borrow my tennis shorts on a Saturday afternoon when I was sixteen, in a scene that appears in *Motherland.*

How did you remember the dialogue, I was asked by a novelist friend.

I checked my notebook, I told her. This does not happen often—that I use thirty-year-old notebooks to corroborate a situation—but when I knew I had to get the dialogue right, I knew where to find it.

But that was never the reason I kept the notebooks in the first place; it was, and is, simply, a compulsion.

These are the things that journals and notebooks can do: they are a private, safe repository for memory and commentary. They keep us honest and are devoid of comparison. Notebook keepers turn over rocks, we swim in the boundary waters between our interior and exterior lives, between dreams and waking life. More than anything, a notebook tests and then ensures our humility, reminding us of our own fragility in a public and creative universe that guarantees stardom as a modern human right. When we remember this, we are left with the promise of grace: that we have used the private page to come to terms with our own questions, our own truths, and have made sense of them.

⁓⦿⁓

Recently, I made the decision to make notebook-keeping a required component in most of my workshops and classes, as a kind of creative anchor, a tether that keeps one honest but also disconnected from the vagaries of the hypercompetitive writing world. I used to know someone whose work sharply mirrored whatever and whoever she was reading at the time: if a person in her life was having quantifiable success writing like Raymond Carver, she would try and write the same way, not necessarily because she was creatively compelled to, but because her art-making was fueled by a fiery competitive urge, an envious streak. It's a common occurrence among makers of art, and anyone who says it isn't is not telling the truth; our humanity comes with all sorts of hiccups and blips and quirks. It only becomes a problem when the competition and envy override one's creative authenticity, which gets eclipsed by the weird, crave-y need born of scarcity mindset to take what someone else has just to keep them from having it; it results in a lazy shadow of the other person's work and an emotional and practical disconnect from one's own. Keeping a notebook *disrupts* this compulsion and the competitive urge to write like anyone but oneself. It is, instead, a place to practice, to experiment, to fiddle, to excavate the truths that drive the words with no one looking over our shoulder.

Although I ask my students to keep a working notebook, it is entirely their choice whether to share what they've written in it, and, if they do, to not share it with any specificity. It is human nature to want to peek between the private covers of other artists, which is why museum and library exhibitions displaying journals and artists' notebooks are so very popular. But in the case of my students, I want to understand not *what* they are thinking, but *how* they are thinking, and how their behind-the-scenes might be informing their on-the-page process, or not. When they choose not to share—most don't share, but for every one who doesn't are ten who believe that their journals are suitable for instant publication—I ask that they think about what they've written privately and how it might affect their creative work. Have they experimented with form? Dug into stories that have never before seen light? Come to understand the core truth of a piece they are writing but are too afraid to reveal publicly?

Permission-to-create touches every part of our lives, be we working artists or not, and almost every creative fear that we have might be diffused—or at least clarified—in the pages of a notebook where we are not writing tentatively. Notebooks are places for practice, for undoing the knots of distraction and shame that keep the work from breathing. Notebooks dilute overwhelm and stick a pin in jealousy and envy: they allow you to pour out whatever it is that needs pouring out, and move on to focus on the work itself.

11

MAKING THE TIME

A writer takes earnest measures to secure his solitude and then finds endless ways to squander it.

—DON DELILLO

W HEN MY father returned home from his service in the navy after the Second World War, he had options afforded him by the GI Bill: he could have gone to university anywhere, but his parents would not allow it and demanded instead that he return home to Brooklyn, to the little bedroom of his childhood. Fearful of being abandoned again, he did what they asked.

At twenty-two, he spent his days working in advertising and his nights getting his degree in business from City College. He wanted to write, he often said, but he couldn't make the time for it. And even when he left after a few tumultuous years— the memory of my grandmother's abandonment infested the apartment—and moved to Canada, he could still not make time for creative work. The writing he longed to do was strangled by grief, and by warnings of shame brought upon the family if people knew the truth; he had taken an unspoken oath of silence. Anything that he might have written would have almost certainly been confessional and revelatory. So creative time slipped through his fingers like sand; when he wasn't working at his corporate job, he was living the life of a New York City bachelor, which involved, in equal measure, Scotch, jazz, museums, women.

But what if he *had* given himself the time, space, and respect to think about his story as one that needed telling, and crafting? Making art from chaos requires *breathing room*—space, air, distance that allows for creative context—enabling us to organize and fathom the *thing that happened*. The amount of time that it takes for a writer to do this is not fixed; it took me years to write a memoir about growing up the daughter of an emotionally abusive, beautiful mother even though I'd been writing shorter pieces about us for years. But our story—the long arc of two lives lived in tandem, aging in parallel—was one that required almost a decade of just *thinking* about it, which is very much part of the process. It may happen quickly for one writer, and not for another. The one thing it does require, though, is self-compassion and respect devoid of judgement, perfection, and shame; with the latter, the crafting of a particularly difficult story may never take place.

We are time-keepers: we set our smartphones to talk to our iPads to talk to our Apple watches to communicate with our laptops in order to keep us on schedule. We have apps that keep us honest about the hours we spend at the gym, or the twenty minutes every morning when we try to meditate. I have two productivity apps downloaded onto my laptop that freeze any ability for me to surf the internet while I'm supposed to be writing, unless I disable them, which I always do. I have triathlete friends who wear special titanium rings that measure the exact number of hours they sleep every night and their heart rate variability, which is an indicator of stress. If they sleep for too many hours, they have to adjust their alarms. Too few hours and they have to go to bed earlier, shielding themselves from all light, including the alarm's blue light that will wake them up.

For a species so hyperscheduled down to the minute, the one thing we cannot seem to do is secure our creative time behind impenetrable boundaries, and treat it with kid gloves, whether that means five, fifteen, or sixty minutes—every day—devoted to our work. We neglect to understand that the act of making art is a sacred one. This is a complicated thing to grasp in a culture that puts the creative act in a tertiary position behind success and money-making (which are not mutually exclusive).

But you don't have children, some of my students tell me.

True.

They are parents, raising children on their own or with a partner. They might be engaged in eldercare, and have an elderly parent living with them; they may be the sandwich generation. Their children may have special needs. They themselves may have special needs. There may be chronic illness requiring regular treatment. Their schedules may be packed.

When the fuck, they ask me, *am I supposed to write?*

This is a complicated question to answer, and a fair one to ask.

I cannot answer it for my students. All I say is this: *if you are here, reading this book, or in my workshop, engaged in doing the generative exercises and the readings, writing is that important to you. You are somehow making time for it, even if you don't know it.*

Every situation is different; every schedule is different; every creative yearning is different. The act of reading, of looking at art, of breathing in the stories that surround you: they are all vital parts of the writing process. If you are a musician—even a not-great one—picking up your guitar on a break from writing is part of the writing process itself. Even if you have no time to get to your desk, you are still engaged in the practice of writing. Art-making is like a spigot that is never, ever turned off.

※

In 1985, a month after I graduated from Boston University, I went to work for the editorial director of a division of Random House, as one of her two editorial assistants. The other one, who

I will call Molly, was a recent Vassar graduate and had been working for the company long before I arrived; she took such an instant dislike to the fact of me that she sabotaged my work, beginning on my first day. We were like the two assistants in *The Devil Wears Prada*: everything I did had to be done twice because my work traveled through her to our boss. Molly took credit for anything of mine that our boss liked, hid manuscripts that I had been instructed to read, and wasted so much of my time that by the end of the day, I was utterly exhausted and demoralized. I was also living with my mother and stepfather on the Upper West Side of Manhattan, going home every night to the leopard print pullout sofa in their den, drinking gargantuan amounts of cheap white wine deep into the night, and fretting over how, when, and where to squeeze my own writing into my days, without luck.

There was another editorial assistant, though, who was working for a different editor, and she seemed to have it all figured out: she wore two large-faced Timex wristwatches on her left wrist, one that reflected actual time and the other, the exact number of hours she would have available to write once she left work and got home to her tiny Greenwich Village apartment. When the alarm on the actual-time watch went off at five P.M., she left work, raced downtown, picked up dinner on the way, dropped her bags just inside her front door, and got to work on what she considered her *real* job: finishing her first novel. When the alarm on that watch went off six hours later, she went to bed, and the whole thing started all over again the next morning.

Some of her colleagues, myself included, thought it an eccentric affectation—she just wanted us all to know that she was a serious writer and would be taking her leave of us as soon as she possibly could—but that wasn't it: she gave her own creative time as much energy, focus, and respect as she gave to the creative time she spent on the work of others, which was how she paid her rent. Every extra minute she had was devoted to either reading or writing, and when the weekends rolled around, she spent them at work on her novel or going to the readings and signing events of other writers whose work she loved. Eventually, though, the schedule began to take its toll, and she gave herself permission to take her work to the next level: she applied for her master of fine arts degree at the University of Iowa Writers' Workshop. She was accepted, and a few years after she graduated, her novel was published and became the first of several; if I revealed her name here, you would likely recognize it. A little while after she left, another of my colleagues, Ann Packer, also went to Iowa for her MFA; her first novel was also published to critical acclaim.

When Ann left Random House to pursue her MFA, I became vaguely ill with an indefinable gastrointestinal problem that left me with daily queasiness. I was still living with my mother and stepfather on their pullout sofa; they wanted to know whether or not I could be pregnant because my nausea occurred every day in the morning, when my alarm clock went off.

I wasn't pregnant; I was green with envy. Envious that these two people had given themselves permission to think of their writing as their *actual* work—beyond the work that paid the bills—and were going to pursue their craft in, arguably, the oldest and best MFA program in the country. They were intentional about their work and the time that it took to make it. They had given themselves *permission* to apply. They had *given themselves permission to take it seriously*, and, presumably, they were supported by the people around them. They had also done one key thing when it comes to art-making: they did it, instead of just talking about it.

Which is not to say that taking one's writing seriously requires an MFA in creative writing—far from it. What it does mean is that devoting time to it in whatever manner you can, and making that time yours—even if it is five minutes a day—is essential to writing.

A year earlier, when I was a senior at Boston University, I began to think of what was next for me: Would I go to law school? (What my mother wanted for me.) Would I get an advanced degree in English and work toward a career in academia? (What my English professors wanted for me.) Would I get an MFA in creative writing? (What my dean wanted for me, and what I wanted for me.)

One day, my father arrived on campus for the weekend, and we drove to Maine for the day to do a little shopping at L. L. Bean. We sat down at a diner to have some lunch.

So what do you think you're going to do after school? my father asked.

I told him: I was thinking of law school, which I really did not want to do. I didn't really want to go into academia at that point, and teaching English at the university level would necessitate a PhD, and I'd spend the next seven years still in school.

I really want, I told him, *to go into an MFA program, to finish a solid piece of work at the end of two years, and to then be able to teach in an MFA program and to write.*

My father stirred his coffee and looked out the window to the parking lot; it was February, and the pavement was wet with slush.

If you go for your MFA, he said, *I will commit suicide.*

I remember the day well; I was wearing a red CB Sports ski jacket and acid-washed jeans tucked into tall duck boots, and a Norwegian ski sweater over a white turtleneck. Vuarnet sunglasses hung around my neck on a robin's-egg-blue Croakie. The booth we were sitting in was red Naugahyde; the table, white marbleized Formica. The plates from which we ate our lunch—I had a grilled-cheese sandwich and a Tab; my father, corned beef on rye and a cup of coffee—were heavy white Buffalo china with a thin green line around the edge.

Time stopped.

My hands trembled. I dug my right index finger nail into the palm of my left hand until it bled.

Why? I whispered.

Because then you could have the insurance money, he said. *And then you could pay for your MFA.*

When my parents divorced in 1978, my father and I clung to each other. We took respite in each other's company, which we both enjoyed without reservation. Ours was a relationship built upon trust and affection, and an unspoken survival of trauma. It was also a life shared in art and music, both of which were of extreme importance in our lives. In wanting to continue my education in the arts, I was doing what he could not allow himself, and what he made the decision to abandon. *Abandonment begets abandonment.*

But my father had also paid for my college education out of pocket; although he barely made enough money to live on, his income on paper was far different from what he brought home, and so we were not eligible for any kind of financial aid. Boston University was a private school, and even in the eighties, one of the most expensive in the country. He did not want me to carry any college debt, nor did he want me to get a work-study job that would offset my tuition. For years, I let myself believe that he thought an MFA would be just another two years of tuition to study what my uncle, an engineer and architect, called *applied phfumphiology*, after which there were no quantifiable guarantees: no financially viable legal career and no teaching license. Just something possibly well written with the possibility, but not probability, of publication. And so, because I loved my father—and because I believed my actions might kill him as he assured me they would; children have a habit of believing their parents when they threaten suicide—I graduated from college and went to work two weeks later, and buried the thought of an MFA somewhere in the recesses of my mind, filed away with other dreams that I recognized as just that: dreams.

It never *once* occurred to me to apply anyway—I was over twenty-one, an adult, and could do what I wanted—and to look for grants and fellowships that would enable me to attend regardless of his feelings on the subject. It never once occurred to me to *own my creative life*, to be responsible for its health and well-being, and its future. My father, who was the most important person in my life at the time, withheld his permission for me to take the earliest steps to fulfill my creative dream, and I would not, and *could not*, give myself permission to apply anyway and to go against his wishes. I could not face the threat of him killing himself because I wanted to not only live a creative life, but to make a career of it. Creativity was nice—I came from a family of practiced artists and musicians—but, I had been taught, frivolous. As children, every one of us—including my cousins, both distant and close—was given music lessons for as long as we wanted them; if we decided to pursue music as a career, the answer was, *No, not for you.*

I adored my father, and it has taken me almost forty years to give myself permission to tell this story about him—to speak it, and to write these words. Exactly two people know about it: my wife, who knew and loved my father, and my Boston University dean, mentor, and dear friend, Linda Wells, who I told thirty-five years after I graduated, while we sat in her darkened suburban Boston living room, drinking tea. She had known my father well as the doting, loving man he mostly was, and a parent deeply involved in his daughter's academic career and future. When I told her —we were talking about regrets and resentments and getting older—she gasped; her mouth fell open in shock.

That might be one of the cruelest, wildest *manipulations I've ever heard one person do to another in order to keep them from fulfilling a creative dream,* she said.

I stifled a guttural groan, the sound an animal would make. Almost four decades of a creative grief so secret and inscrutable threatened to overtake me. I had a classic trauma response: my feet went numb and then my hands, and I jumped up, nervously, to leave, hugged her goodbye, sat in my car, and wept until I could barely see.

I've tried, over the years, to peel the onion—to truly capture the core of what made my father say what he did that gray afternoon in Maine, and I have finally come to this: he tried to commit *creative filicide.* He was a successful advertising executive and creative director who, after repeated rejections for his rhyming poetry and his short, sometimes ribald pieces that were knotted with tortured, flowery language, had given up any hope of being a writer; the one story that my father *had to* tell—about surviving and transcending childhood abandonment—he could not, and would not, lest he risk another familial abandonment. My father did not love the possibility that I might become a writer, and that I took it seriously enough to consider it and respected the fact of it; that I longed for the time in which to write in an MFA environment where all I was expected to do was produce words. Certainly, it was partly the money; he probably assumed that I expected him to pay for it, which I didn't.

But he never said, *If you get accepted, you'll have to find a way to pay for it yourself.*

He said, *I'll commit suicide.*

A codependent snare; a paralyzing trap.

In Rick Rubin's *The Creative Act*, the author writes in the clearest terms about the practice of art-making. He touches on all of it: collaboration, distraction, nature as setting, patience, and time as it relates to the natural rhythms of art-making. Annie Dillard reduces time to a marker of focus or waste, and writes in *The Writing Life, How we spend our days is how we spend our lives. What we do with this hour and that one is what we are doing.* Virginia Woolf comes closer to defining the link between art-making and time: *A woman must have money and a room of her own if she is to write fiction.* And here we are faced with a quandary: money and a room of one's own are synonymous here with time and freedom. Wealthy (usually white) women who are afforded the time and space to create will do so; women who are not will almost always struggle. Tillie Olsen, one of the greatest feminist writers of the twentieth century, received a Random House book contract in response to an excerpt of a novel chapter she published in the *Partisan Review* in 1934; she abandoned it because of the demands made on her time as a mother and manager of her household, and she didn't publish her first book until 1961, at almost fifty, well after her children were grown. A familiar story, echoed by more woman artists than can be counted on a city's-worth of fingers, including Doris Lessing, who made the decision to leave two of her three children behind in nineteen fifties Rhodesia and move to London, where she believed her writing career would be better supported; she was pilloried for this choice until the day she died. Buried in the transcriptions of poet Anne Sexton's taped therapy sessions from 1961–1964 is the incendiary line *Writing is as important as my children.* Claire Dederer, in her book *Monsters,* refers to women—Alice Walker, Jean Rhys, and others—who *self-split* in order to balance or *not* balance their lives as mothers and creatives as *the divided self.* My grandmother's decision to leave her family in 1926 for what I conjecture was the promise of a creative life was *the divided self* in action; her returning a dissatisfied artist and mother who would be scorned for her actions the rest of her days rendered her silent, squelched, playing Chopin etudes on her lap in her sleep.

I knew her as kind and loving, devoted to her family, yet frustrated. My grandmother from the old country was microcosmic; she was probably representative of the millions of other creative women devoted to their art, whose lives and stories will never be known. Recently, I shared her story with two colleagues and speculated over her leaving, and why she did: the woman answered, cutting me off.

For the sake of art, she said.

The man answered, *Because she was a monster.*

* * *

In the writer's workshops I lead, one of the most significant challenges my students, who are mostly women, face is *time*. My younger students are often working full-time jobs that, even after the pandemic, involve significant commutes. Students who are slightly older are often new mothers faced with the challenges of working, nursing, feeding themselves, and inevitably being charged with the running of their households. Single mothers work full-time jobs—at least one, in many cases—after shuttling their children off to preschool or daycare and then picking them up, making dinner, and putting them to bed. Mothers of teens are faced with the problems that every soccer mom deals with: getting one child to one event and another to another event, getting everyone fed, cleaned, put to bed. Members of the sandwich generation are taking care of teenagers and elderly parents simultaneously. In my own case, I spend an unpredictably large number of hours each day taking care of an elderly, unwell mother living in another state: I spend my days ordering and having her food delivered, her medication monitored, her aide managed, her rent paid, her laundry done, her house kept clean, all while fielding the (often fourteen) phone calls she makes to me every day, to chat. Forget how one finds time to paint, or draw, or design. One must find the time, simply, *to take a breath.*

How do artists find time to even *think* about their creative lives without exhausting oneself, or feeling guilty, or being made to feel guilty, for taking time away from their families? By giving oneself permission to *make* the time—to take the time with neither guilt nor reticence nor the demand by others to quantify it—to focus on the art-making to which they are drawn. Years ago, pulled from pillar to post with work and eldercare and my own health concerns, I began doing two things every morning, no matter what: meditating for fifteen minutes and writing for ten minutes in a journal. Regardless of my schedule or whether or not I wanted to get out of bed (I hate getting out of bed), I went into the guest room before sunup, closed the door behind me, and sat on a meditation cushion. When my timer went off, I wrote for ten minutes. Eventually, it became like muscle memory, and I just rolled out of bed and into the guest room and did it without thinking about it; my wife called it *grooving a new habit*. When my schedule became even more stretched, I could barely find time to walk around the block; I became paralyzed with the anxiety that stole my personal creative time, and my new habit fell away. I didn't give those few minutes every morning—just ten: maybe the amount of time we spend in the shower—priority. If I had, no one would have been able to take it away: not my spouse, not my mother, not my other deadlines. Ten minutes; that's all it was, and I couldn't even manage that.

What most of us forget is that creative time does *not need* to be spent in active practice; when, for example, my students tell me that they haven't been able to find time to write but they *are* reading—during their train or bus commute, in bed, at lunch—they're surprised when I tell them that this counts as *active creative time*. When the artist Maira Kalman wants to be creatively stimulated, she says, she puts down her paintbrush, puts on her coat, and goes for a walk around Greenwich Village, where she lives, and walks while paying attention to the people who are moving around her. In conversation with the host of *Design Matters*, Debbie Millman, Kalman also described being completely compelled by reading the obituaries every morning in the *New York Times* (which is something that my own father used to do, daily, he said, to make sure he was still alive). At least one of those obituaries bore creative fruit: Kalman found the 2001 obituary for Megan Boyd, a Scottish fish fly master so captivating—the headline read "Eccentric Master of Fish Flies, Dies at 86"—that she painted Boyd according to the description in the paper: *A man's shirt and tie, sweater, wool skirt, tweed sport jacket and heavy army-style boots. But the flies she dressed at a small table in front of a window and under a gas lamp . . . were regarded by connoisseurs as 'the Tiffanies of the 20ᵗʰ century.'* Awarded a British Empire Medal by Queen Elizabeth, Boyd explained to the Palace that she couldn't take the time to come down to London for the ceremony from Golspie, Scotland, where she lived, because she didn't have anyone to take care of her dog that day. No one gave her permission to say no, and she didn't ask for it. We do not know what the royal response was. If there was grace involved, which I hope there was, it calls to mind Rilke's words: *I hold this to be the highest task of a bond between two people: that each should stand guard over the solitude of the other.*

A friend who lives in small-town conservative East Texas is well known by her social media moniker Sober Vegan Cop. An anomaly where she lives, she awakens every morning at four to go to the gym, come home and write for an hour in a space she's created just for that purpose, shower and put on her uniform, and feed her three kids. She has made her creative time precious and hers, and it is an understood fact in her home. Anne Lamott, in conversation with her son Sam, an author, podcaster, and artist, describes how, on a given Sunday—after church, after her daily walk, after corralling the husband and the grandson and the grandson's friends and the dog and the cat—she steps into her office, closes the door, and writes for an hour and a half. Come hell or high water. When Sam asks her about it, she answers with one word: *boundaries.*

In the case of Maira Kalman, her mundane reading of the paper is *still* creative time, emblematic of the fact that inspiration exists everywhere we look, assuming we are not too distracted to notice it. For my Sober Vegan Cop friend in Texas (who has not yet published a word) and for Anne Lamott (who has written twenty books), the rules are the same: Prioritize creative time. Slow things down; breathe. Give yourself one minute and then two and then three; take it as yours and yours alone, and make it inviolable.

The time I spend writing requires, like Anne's, boundaries. My cell phone is silenced and often left in another room. I ignore the pull to check my email just once more. If necessary, I leave my home office and go somewhere I can work uninterrupted. (As I write this, I am sitting at a very generous friend's dining room table in her empty house in Maine.) Even if all I have is a single hour in which to write, I now take it, when I used to feel guilty about it, and about saying, *I will be unreachable for this period of time.*

What was the switch that got flipped? The realization that even the most wonderful people in the world often do not and cannot acknowledge and respect boundaries. They will call my cell, send me emails, call my watch (Lord have mercy), send me a text saying, *I know you're busy but I just have this one question I have to ask you.* Unless someone needs to know my blood type because they are in need of an immediate transfusion, it is not an emergency; it can wait. I have recently taken to putting up out-of-office messages so that when someone emails me, they know that I'm not ignoring them, that I'm at work—*this is my work; please respect that*—and I will be in touch when I'm done. And yet: push, they must.

At core, permission to take creative time for oneself is directly connected to intentionality, meaning *intention as it relates to art,* to the practice of creation and art-making with resolution and purpose—not to necessarily create something that will be commodified. Without time to create, we move through the world robotically, from job to job, place to place, event to event.

Creative time is a gift we give ourselves that we can never expect will come from someone or somewhere else; this is part of what makes it so guilt-inducing. We are trained from our first breath to be recipients of bequeathment and approval from others: they allow us the time by their good graces, for which we are meant to be formally—and often publicly—grateful.

12

THE MAGIC IN
THE MUNDANE

Normalize the incredible.

—MARY KARR

A LL OF our stories are at once large and small, and bound up in beauty and in pain; this is the human condition. *To be loving,* wrote bell hooks, *is to be open to grief, to be touched by sorrow, even sorrow that is unending.* This is the nature of interiority. To close oneself off to this grief—to refrain from creative lament that might transform experience from destruction and trauma to revelation—is to also close oneself off from joy, to separate oneself from humanity, to don creative armor that we believe, mistakenly, will protect our creative souls and spirits. Instead, it causes paralysis.

My father's desire—his hunger and *need*—to write was flattened by grief, by familial warnings that forced him to make a choice, either consciously or not: tell his story about his mother's abandonment and how this experience forever altered his worldview until he drew his final breath, or maintain the silence and the myth of perfection constructed by his tiny household sheathed in shame. He held back from writing memoir because grappling with his story in any public way was likely unimaginable for him; it would have required a reliving of it on the one hand, and going against his family's requirement to put the past behind him on the other. To fulfill his creative yearning would have been a risky proposition, conceivably resulting in more abandonment. He chose, instead, to tell the story of his mother's leaving over and over to me like a biblical warning, unaware that I would ever write about it; it worked its way into every one of our conversations, making me collateral damage. *You take yourself with you, wherever you go,* wrote Stephen King's narrator in *Doctor Sleep,* his sequel to *The Shining,* in which Danny Torrance, now an adult and an alcoholic, begins to attend recovery meetings, finding that memories are *the real ghosts*. Meaning: you will carry your story with you forever, and inescapably. As Claudia Rankine writes in *Citizen: The world is wrong. You can't put the past behind you. It's buried in you; it's turned your flesh into its own cupboard. Not everything remembered is useful but it all comes from the world to be stored in you.*

And yet, the world we live in demands that our experiences be extraordinary, exceptional, large. *My story is bigger than yours. My story is shinier than yours. My story is more outrageous than yours.* We are faced with this requirement every day of our lives, wherever we turn. On social media, we see people who are more beautiful, younger, funnier, more successful. They live in houses that are perfect, with perfect, white-tiled, marble-topped kitchens and perfect light-splashed bathrooms, perfect raised-bed gardens growing perfect vegetables that could win contests for their sheer size alone. They have better hair. They drive bigger, faster cars, run longer distances, compete in more marathons, lift heavier weights, make healthier smoothies, have the intermittent fasting thing down pat, meditate every morning at five, the malas they were gifted by the Tibetan lama they've studied with for years in hand.

If we look beyond the exteriority of their lives and their Stuff, we can actually see who people are and how they present themselves to the world, which is also why a lot of people are so attracted to Instagram and Facebook and TikTok: these are places where so-called ordinary people can safely set up a socially acceptable *them versus you* scenario in which their job is better, their visibility bigger, their skin clearer, the awards they've won more exclusive and important. They've recovered from bigger traumas, overcome the worst possible addictions, led workshops packed with hundreds of students who want to know their secrets. We applaud them, give them likes or perhaps even loves, congratulate them, and then, assuming we are human, we try not to drink to excess or stick our heads in our ovens out of a combination of envy and distraction, which in turn serve to do one thing and one thing only: make us feel less than, deflate us, pull us away from our own work. Because every person who engages in *us versus them* behavior on social media, or in their work, or in their extended families—how many of us have the obnoxious cousin who is forever trying to outdo her own relatives on Thanksgiving—is doing so because of the scarcity mindset that says: *I have to take what is yours even if I myself don't want it because less for you means more for me. So don't even bother.*

To them I ask: What is the *nugget* of their story? Where is the mundanity in their lives that, when rendered as narrative, will make their experience universally relatable? How stunningly human is it? Or does exceptionalism lurk beneath the surface of everything they do, everything they are, because of the perfection that was demanded of them as children?

My story isn't important enough to tell, my students say. *I didn't hike the Pacific Coast Trail,* they add, *or overcome a heroin addiction, or flee a cult, or go through gender transition while growing up in a right-wing neofascist family. I didn't struggle as a member of a marginalized group, or live through a genocide. I grew up white and middle class in the suburbs with a house and a dog and parents, and a grandmother who lived in the small sewing room at the top of the stairs.*

What story will you write, then, if it is not yours? I ask. *How will you tell your story if it is not enough to look at it via its texture, its color, its sound?*

They shake their heads, embarrassed that the thing they want to tell is just too mundane—*too boring,* they say—to be of interest to anyone. I'm reminded of a test used by some editors deciding whether to acquire a book. They read a sentence and say, *So what?* Another one, *and so what?* My students ask it themselves: *Who would care? Why bother?*

Peek beyond the surface of your ordinary story, I tell them: *Does Grandma carry a flask of blackberry brandy in her housecoat pocket? Does the dog have a habit of relieving himself on the father's pillow every morning as a thank-you for the secret beatings? Does Mom put on her lipstick whenever the FedEx guy is driving down the street?*

Peel back the layers of humanity, and begin your early draft from the most mundane of places. Don't be afraid to get granular, and sensory. Imagine: the smell of cigar smoke, or maybe cannabis, on your doctor's hands. Chopping onions with your grandmother's dull cleaver, which she carried over from the old country. The mysterious lock of hair found in your father's wallet by the emergency room nurse when they brought him in after the accident.

One of the most chilling pieces I have ever read about permission to write arrived in a popular how-to-write-and-get-published newsletter. There, buried at the bottom of the page, was a question-and-answer section containing a letter from an eighty-year-old woman asking if she should bother to write her memoir given her advanced age. The answer from the editor contained much wisdom about joy in process, and ended with, *So I would ask, again, why you want to write this memoir. What kind of impact do you want to make, and on whom? And, once you've articulated those answers in some detail, maybe there's another question to ask, which is whether writing a memoir is the only way to tell the stories you want to tell.*

The implication in the answer is that storytelling—that any art-making—must always be a means to an end: measuring *impact on others* is important during the publishing process, but not during writing, unless the thing being written is a textbook or a self-help guide. Telling a new writer, however old they may be, that *impact* on others needs to be a consideration during their writing process is like telling a painter to stick strictly to commercial art. Impact on others is just another form of perceived value, of market viability, neither of which should have anything to do with whether someone should choose to create or not. *Impact on others* is a trip wire, a snare that has stopped more creatives in their tracks than perhaps anything else. There *is* no impact on others unless and until the art is made.

Asking someone to consider *impact on others* too early in the process is another example of forcing comparison as a result of valuation; we fall prey to the belief that louder is better and bigger is more important. We hold ourselves and our stories up against those of others on social media who call themselves *influencers. Why bother to write at all if their story is so much better, so much more interesting,* we ask ourselves.

But, as Krista Tippett has often remarked: loud doesn't always win. Virginia Woolf, in *To the Lighthouse*, said it best: *The great revelation perhaps never did come. Instead there were little daily miracles, illuminations, matches struck unexpectedly in the dark.* Honor the mundane, then; pay attention to the daily miracles and create art from that place of the gorgeously routine, where the work that is created is emblematic of the human condition. *Normalize the incredible,* because the normal is incredible, for every one of us. Resist the urge for the hyperbolic, the excessive, the extreme, the shocking. Resist the exclamation point; let the words and the story do the work. Rake the mulch off the fabulous; look beneath its surface and turn over its stones and dig around in its leaves.

During the creative process, keep *impact on others* at a long arm's length.

In the most mundane stories lie humanity. It is where the magic is, where the stories lurk, where the most stunning and affecting art is waiting to be made. It is here where joy and sorrow and the absurd and the human are plaited together in a tight braid, and, as Donald Hall wrote, where *grief's repeated particles suffuse the air.*

In Mary Karr's first memoir, *The Liars' Club*, the narrator and her sister, Lecia, are asked by a contractor redoing their mother's kitchen about the cause of a hole in an old tile he pries from the wall.

Now Miss Karr, the contractor says to the author's mother, *this looks like a bullet hole.*

Mother, isn't that where you shot at daddy? asks Lecia.

Their mother, reading a copy of Marcus Aurelius and eating a bowl of chili, responds, *No, that's where I shot at Larry . . . Over there's where I shot at your daddy.*

The conversation unfolds as though it was an everyday chat, and nothing out of the ordinary, which it probably wasn't. A normalizing of the incredible, made even more mundane by the eating of the chili, the Aurelius.

In Virginia Woolf's *Mrs. Dalloway*, a middle-aged woman goes out to buy flowers for a party that she is going to have that night. Mundane. It is only when the onion is peeled and the story begins to unfold like a lotus blossom that we see—first microscopically, then very clearly—how tenuous the lives of the characters are.

Mrs. Dalloway and *The Liars' Club* could not be more different, beyond the fact that, at core, their foundation is witheringly trau-matic. One story is fiction, and the other, memoir. And yet, the two stories are entrenched in the ordinary lives of ordinary peo-ple who, if one scratches the surface, are not ordinary at all. This is the universal condition that we forget amidst the glories and soft filters of social media: *no human life is ordinary*, nor is any story. Let's see the lines and the age, the lives lived, the weeds overtaking the garden, the successes and the failures, the men-tal illnesses and the addictions, the quiet cruelties perpetrated by the tidiest of people. Let's see the tiny immigrant woman who doesn't come home one night before the Great Depression while her husband and children are waiting for her: Had she left din-ner in the oven? Made her bed? Were there instructions on when to bathe her toddler son, and how he liked his eggs? Let's see them as they are in all their brilliant mundane clarity.

Forget perfectionism: the mundane *reeks* of imperfection, and that imperfection is what makes for beauty of a human sort, as opposed to the fabricated, inauthentic sort.

In a conversation with Krista Tippett, the poet Marie Howe recounts the first time she meets new students, and the exercise she gives them every week. *List ten things that you saw today,* she tells them; they come back to her the next week with their list of things, dripping with flowery metaphor. Describing what one sees, and describing it plainly, is a complex business. Where's the trap? In seeing things as they are, as opposed to the way we imagine they might be. The trap is being willing to see the mun-dane and the plain, and the absolute beauty that exists in them, which is far greater than any Instagram-filtered life might have you believing it is.

* * *

When I began painting my shitty little watercolors, I wanted to paint vast canvases that were instantly frameable, that held great meaning, were salable. I wanted my rendering of Monhegan Island to look like Edward Hopper's and Andrew Wyeth's; instead, it looked like Lassie's, if Lassie could paint.

Start small, my wife, who is a visual artist, said. *Just paint what you see, and what is in your line of vision. Why do you think painters start with still lifes—with bowls of fruit and cups of tea? What could be more mundane than that?*

But what about expectations? What about comparison? What about *impact on others?* What about the noise, and the fact that people not only like to look at amazing things and pretty pictures and bright and shiny objects, and read wild stories of transcendence and overcoming the most extraordinary and overwhelming of problems—they *expect* to?

Years ago, I stopped into the New York Road Runner's offices on West Fifty-Seventh Street in Manhattan; it was November, and just before the marathon was going to start. A few feet from where runners would come in and pick up their race numbers was a shop selling jackets and T-shirts to the public, emblazoned with the words MARATHON FINISHER. One didn't have to train, or even run (or even walk, for that matter); one could just buy, for twenty-five dollars, a cotton shirt that would proclaim its wearer an exceptional athlete who had persevered through hundreds of hours of exhausting training, who had sweated, devoted themselves to completing the event, lost their toenails, and gone home with a finisher's medal. Even when they hadn't. Because *expertise* and the *exceptional* can be had for a price: one can leap right over process, right over human story, right over what the Bhagavad Gita calls duty—do your duty and don't concern yourself with the results—and land on INCREDIBLE. As opposed to the skinny seventy-something man in Maine who runs up and down my street by the ocean every morning, wearing an old, tattered, seventies Penn singlet and beat-up Tiger running shoes that date back to the Clinton administration. *Who is he? Why does he run? Did he go to Penn? What is his story?* Indigenous American marathoner Billy Mills said that the *number one objective of his Olympic pursuit was to heal a broken soul.* This is his story, unbuyable on a T-shirt, unobtainable for any price.

This is what I share with my students early on, and at first, they're not happy about it because we are hardwired to aim for quantifiable success; it doesn't thrill them because of the inherent ego that every art-maker has. *When you're living a creative life— when you've given yourself permission to be an art-maker, to tell the story, to paint the painting, to sing the song, to bead the necklace— you don't get to first think about whether or not it will be successful in the world, or in the open marketplace.* You don't get to wonder if your story is exciting enough to rattle the chains of your millions of readers who will race to the nearest airport bookstore to buy your book because everyone else is indefinitely out of stock until they go back to press with a nice big fat tenth printing. You don't get to do that. Because that is not what art-making is about; also, you're not there yet. This is not your life, at least not for now. There are anomalies, certainly. But art-making is, by its nature, a solitary and spiritual practice. *To accept the fruits of these things as gifts is to acknowledge that we are not their owners or masters, that we are, if anything, their servants, their ministers,* wrote Lewis Hyde in *The Gift.* Authentic art-making, then, cannot be about leaping over the sweat of the process—the work, the sleepless nights, the exuberance when a core truth about our work comes to us at three in the morning out of a dream—to a place of preconceived success. We do not get to be marathon finishers unless we've run the race.

One needs to divorce oneself from the end result—what it might or might not be—and instead to focus on the now, on the work, the craft, on seeing what one sees, learning what one learns, without judging it as boring or thrilling or bad or good. Only in that way are we able to transcend the demon voices that tell us that we have no story to tell, and no meaning behind our words.

My father grew up in a family of loving and kind perfectionists, who taught him that meticulous pedantry was a sure way to a shame-free existence; he had been warned about writing his story of surviving abandonment as a small boy because it would lead to evidence of the family's self-perceived inferiority as immigrants who had fled the shtetls of Europe for the supposed riches of America, only to be hobbled by dishonor once they arrived. Unable to write his story because of the trauma, the shame, the directive never to speak of it—*a mother walks out, returns four years later, and it impacts generations to come*—he was limited to composing solipsistic rhyming poetry and, after reading Philip Roth and Frank O'Connor, a few libidinous bits of short fiction, all of which were shoehorned into the overwritten shape of the pieces he read in *Playboy* and *Esquire*. They were meant to wow editors into publishing his work; they never did.

Poet Donald Hall is quoted in Peter Makuck's *Sewanee Review* essay on poetry and ambition: Hall writes that *for almost every poet it is necessary to live in exile before returning home—an exile rich in conflict and confirmation . . . [Certain places] may shine at the center of our work and lives; but if we never leave these places, we are not likely to grow up enough to do the work.*

My father would have had to *leave these places* of shame and secrecy to tell his own deeply human, beautifully mundane story of loss and love, resilience and healing. As a creative, I believe that he was meant to. But he couldn't; he was not given permission to, nor could he give it to himself.

Pay attention; the magic in the mundane is everywhere. On a steaming April day, I wandered into a Corsicana, Texas, vintage shop owned by a middle-aged woman. I was in the small Texas town for a month-long writing fellowship, and after a morning of work, I decided to go out for a walk. I have a thing for vintage shops, I'd never been to Texas, and I had visions of finding the perfect pair of old suede cowboy boots, or a snap-front Western yoked shirt, or a beautifully faded pair of Wranglers worn by a cowboy/cowgirl/cowperson. The woman, blond and heavily made-up, smiled and said, *Hiyahoney,* and nervously glanced down at her watch, which was the type that someone's grandmother might have worn back in the sixties: a tiny face, gold, on an elastic gold band that was stretched to its limit.

Are you closing? I asked. *Because I can come back later—*

No, honey, she said. *I'm just worried about the turtles—*

Okay, I'll bite, I thought.

Turtles?

Yeah, honey, she said. *In the pool—*

You have turtles in the pool? I asked.

(It was not just a pool; it was *the* pool, and there is a difference. It's important to listen for narrative differences like that.)

While we chatted, I browsed her bookshelf, which held everything from a used hardcover copy of Stephen King's *The Stand* to an ancient paperback edition of Leo Rosten's *The Joys of Yiddish*.

Oh yeah, she said. *I forgot to clean it out last year and when I went to shock it with the chemicals a few months back, there was a family of turtles in it—*

What did you do? I asked, taking a book off the shelf.

I fed them. And I named 'em, she said, taking a set of keys out of her purse. *The big one's Albert.*

Albert—

Course I don't know if it's a girl or not, she said, shrugging.

Of course, I said.

I brought the book up to the counter—it was a first edition hardcover copy of the *I Ching,* the corner of page 351 folded down and a section of it highlighted in fading fluorescent pink marker: *Chapter X: The Changes is a book vast and great, in which everything is completely contained. The tao of heaven is in it, the tao of the earth is in it, and the tao of man is in it.*

I gave her a five-dollar bill.

Thanks for coming by, honey, she said, taking the money. She shut the lights off, we walked out together to the street, and she locked the door.

The story I began to write on the short walk back to my residence: *a middle-aged storekeeper, maybe a former high school homecoming queen going through a divorce forgets to clean her pool which turns into a fetid swamp that births a family of turtles who become her pets. The pool: the tao of heaven is in it, the tao of the earth is in it, and the tao of man is in it.*

Story is everywhere. The magic is *always* in the mundane, if we pay attention and turn over the stones of excess and exceptionalism. And *attention,* as Mary Oliver said, *is the beginning of devotion.*

13

GENEROSITY OF SPIRIT

Perhaps all the dragons in our lives are
princesses who are only waiting to see us
act, just once, with beauty and courage.

—RAINER MARIA RILKE

THE CREATIVE act requires bravery, time, a willingness to listen to an evanescent command that might be as fleeting as a breeze.

I once had a well-known novelist show up in one of my memoir workshops, along with someone who had never written before. They both expressed the same thing in the same way, regardless of their experience: memoir frightened them. No matter who we are, the impulse to make art is equal parts primal need and paralyzing fear. If we intend to share our art, we will be judged. If we don't intend to share our art, we will still judge ourselves and compare our work to the work of others. *Will what we make be deemed good? Will it be ravaged, or worse, met with flat ambivalence? If we're writing memoir or personal essay, will we anger someone we're writing about? Will we reveal secrets?* Permission to create—the willingness to bequeath ourselves the psychic, emotional, actual time and space to do our work—requires a generosity of spirit and respect not only from others, *but from ourselves.* And in a modern, capitalist world that has a complicated relationship with art-making for its own sake and disconnected from any kind of remuneration, this self-respect is both a necessary requirement and a promise to oneself that requires compassion.

Who we are—how we respond and react to the world around us—changes day by day (and, if the news is dire, minute by minute); some days are bad, and some days are good. Some days the phone won't stop ringing; some days we get sucked into the vortex of comparison that is social media, and we become our own worst enemies. And because every day is different, any artist engaged in creative practice will tell you this truth: we put down the pen or the paintbrush in the early evening, as the light through our studio window is beginning to dim, and the next day, when we return to our work—assuming we do—we will rarely view it in the same way or from the same point of view. But we must, no matter what, start out with the belief, as poet Brenda Hillman said, that we are *entitled to write.*

The practicalities of the matter: when I sit down at my desk after twelve hours and an overnight away—maybe I was away teaching; maybe I was taking care of my mother in another state, with whom I have had lifelong, epic conflict akin to that of a Greek tragedy—it takes me a while to return to the previous day's work groove and even longer to become entrenched in it in any kind of a generative way. Some writers believe in keeping one's rear in their office chair and staring at their computer screen until something emerges; one writer friend demands this of herself and her students, whether or not it is quantifiably productive. Another says she keeps bankers' hours, whether she wants to or not. I have nothing but the most profound respect for these people, but I'm also skeptical of such requirements because life is hard enough without setting ourselves up for possible failure. Because when we fail, we also often stop working. I believe that creative stringency and dogma results in a kind of nervous tic borne of self-flagellation when the words *don't* come, and very often, they don't.

That said, there is no on/off switch in the creative act. We are creative sponges, always thinking, always working, always reading, always absorbing, always looking at art, always looking at the people around us and at the natural world. Unlike other kinds of work, creative inspiration comes when it comes; for our part, we have to be ready for it, and recognize it when it nudges us to pay attention. *Be a good steward of your gifts,* wrote Jane Kenyon.

Protect your time. Feed your inner life. Avoid too much noise. Read good books, have good sentences in your ear. Be by yourself as often as you can. Walk. Take the phone off the hook. Work regular hours. Meaning: the creative life is composed of more than pen-on-paper, or brush-on-canvas. We must be open to the world around us and recognize—with radical compassion for ourselves and the lives we lead—when our subject is speaking to us, where, and how.

Radical creative self-compassion in practice looks like anything—and any ritual—that enables you to harness and foster your own creative energy without apology or guilt: Haruki Murakami runs a daily 10K in the afternoons when he is working on a novel; Terry Tempest Williams is known to light a candle on her desk to mark the moment when she begins to work; Anne Lamott, whose home often resembles a lovely three-ring circus filled with her grandson and his friends, her son, her husband, friends, and pets, steps into her writing space and closes the door behind her for an hour and a half, without explanation; John Cheever's creative ritual involved orgasm for the work to take off; if I hit a creative roadblock, I play the guitar for exactly half an hour, no more and no less, and no singing because someone else's words are a distraction.

My own rituals have emerged over the many years during which I've been writing: creative compassion requires that I retype or transcribe the last thousand words I wrote just so that my brain re-enters the same space with the same rhythm and the same cadence, the same narrative sensibility that I left behind the day before; this is my practice and my process. The creative human mind is anchored in *pattern recognition*, and returning to the work of the day before can be likened to a good stretch before a race; the body is called upon to remember how it is supposed to move, and why. Many writers do this or a version of it; Joan Didion described returning to her work every day in this manner. This is creative self-compassion in action: the art-maker gives themselves permission to take the work seriously enough to *re-enter it*, to give it time and energy.

Pay attention. Be astonished. Tell about it. When Mary Oliver wrote these words in her collection *Red Bird*, she unwittingly created a clarion call for all those art-makers who applied the word *generosity* to others rather than oneself. *Pay attention* is a directive, borne of the requirement of generosity turned Inward. *Pay attention* is an order that requires the heart be involved in the work. And the heart is always involved in the work. *Let me keep my mind on what matters / which is my work / which is mostly standing still and learning to be astonished,* writes Oliver in her poem "Messenger." It is impossible to experience self-compassion and generosity of spirit and to not stand still and learn; *attention*, Oliver wrote, *is the beginning of devotion.* Devotion—to the world, to work, to one's art—comes from within, and only from within.

Naturalist and author of *Silent Spring* Rachel Carson wrote, *The discipline of the writer is to learn to be still and listen to what his subject has to tell him.* This getting quiet and listening is imperative in a world built upon a foundation of noise. But it also does not mean that what is produced as a result is always worthy of publication; it just means that stillness and devotion together sift out the dust and detritus from new work and make room for what will stay.

14

TRUTH AND BEAUTY

How alive am I willing to be?

—ANNE LAMOTT

WHAT IS it that separates a well-crafted memoir from one that lacks humanity?

Among other things: a sense of ambiguity, of imperfection—physical, moral, ethical—among its characters, and the knowledge that even the wisest, most handsome, charismatic of people might have moments of profound assholery that need to appear on the page. Likewise, we must allow the rogues in our stories to emerge with some whiff of humanity, even if it is fleeting. Fagin in Dickens's *Oliver Twist* is widely viewed as a villain based on the worst of anti-Semitic tropes: he's a wily thief, a pickpocket, a money-grubber. And yet: he is the only home, the only kindness, the only stability—wobbly though it is—that his throng of young bandits will ever know.

The idea that every story must be tied up with a nice little ribbon—*and they all lived happily ever after*—is a myth perpetrated on the creative community by Hollywood, and the gentle fairy tales that many of us grew up with. When a story, be it fictional or true, is wrapped up like a neat little package at its end, all it is succeeding in doing is insulting the reader's intelligence with the belief that we go through trial and trauma, and once the glass slipper fits, we marry the prince. This is not real; it's a Nancy Meyers movie.

If I get too entrenched in telling the story of a particular character—myself included—I have to take a step back and ask myself whether or not I'm being accurate. *Truthful.* Is what I'm writing more than a lazy, one-dimensional attempt at storytelling where characters and situations live on the binary planet of All Good or All Bad? Truth and beauty are a narrative necessity. The former bears the latter, and together they comprise the fundamental fuel for art-making.

The truth: *every one of us is a human being, with all our petti-ness and love, jealousy and generosity, kindness and schadenfreude.* The beauty: *the very fact of our imperfect humanity is what makes art transcendent on the visceral and spiritual level.*

In my longer memoir workshops—the ones that go on for a month, or even ten weeks—one of the generative exercises I give my students is this: write a thousand-word description of your narrator from the point of view of another character who is in conflict with them (and conflict does not always have to trans-late to battle; it just means that they are somehow at odds). If the character has a bone to pick with the narrator, let's see it. If the character is keeping a secret about the narrator because she's been told to, let's understand it. If the character once loved the narrator, tell us why they don't anymore. I assign this exercise at the midway point in the workshop because, for the most part, the students have spent the entire first half of the class writing strictly from the point of view of the narrator, and not only can they not see their own narrator's fallibility and cunning: they don't want to. Who would? This exercise is like putting on well-worn shoes belonging to someone else; they've already been molded and shaped to someone else's feet, with its bunions and calluses and hammertoes, and they feel completely alien to you.

The hurdle in this exercise is that the narrator is the *on-the-page character representing the author*—you—and so I have asked that the tables be turned, and that all the blips and hic-cups and latent personality quirks that lie beneath the surface of the narrator's persona must come to the fore through the eyes of someone else. What I am asking: what does this particular character—the one you might eventually go head-to-head with—actually think of you?

There is no wrong way to do this, provided that the students are actually willing to peek under their own hoods. It can be anything: *Does the narrator scrape the side of their cereal bowl every morning—three times; no more, no less—and it drives the other character crazy and has for thirty-two years? Does the character know something about the narrator that they will hold against him? Is the narrator's innate arrogance the thing that destroyed their relationship?*

It can also be far more mundane: *How does this other character tolerate the narrator's complex grief, and inability to seek help for it? What does the character think of the narrator's choice of jeans?*

Inevitably, three or four people in every workshop simply do not *get* the exercise; they will overcomplicate it, torture it, turn it inside out. They will almost always have the character describe someone *other* than the narrator. Or they will leave things superficial and write, *I think that the narrator is very nice.* One student, whose work was limited to repeated declarations of her own physical beauty and astonishing prowess in bed, simply swapped pronouns when writing from the point of view of her ex-husband: *He thinks I am so stunning and our sex life is wonderful because he is so overwhelmed by my beauty* became *I think she is so stunning and our sex life is wonderful because I am overwhelmed by her beauty.*

The inability of the writer to move beyond the flat, one-dimensional safety of their own descriptions is a refusal to let go of the side of the pool. They maintain a vise grip on their own veneer, their own perfect personhood. They want their reader to think what they want them to think, feel what they want them to feel, cry when they want them to cry. They are pulling the reins this way and that. This refusal to allow the reader to come to their own opinions about their narrator runs contrary to what makes for good memoir: ambiguity. *Let the reader come to understand who the narrator is without being told who they are by the narrator*: this is the craft of writing, and represents the good, true work that excavates the soul of a story, and separates it from that which is dogged by creative insecurity on one hand, and martyrdom on the other.

What makes the exercise complicated is that I am asking the writer to look at who they are through the eyes of someone else, and to do so subjectively and personally. *The loneliness of the monster and the cunning of the innocent,* in Vivian Gornick's words. What results from this exercise: compassion for the narratorial self and empathy for the other character, the latter of which may not have existed previously.

※

Humans are humans, though, and, as my family's story shows, we have a vested interest in patinas that are specifically designed to keep our reputations neat and shiny; we do everything we can to create burnished personas for ourselves that are designed to be more attractive, exciting, fabulous, be it for our friends and loved ones or our colleagues. Conversely, that burnished persona that we fashion for ourselves can implode in a split second: we now live in a world of constant (over)exposure, and the acts of ghosting, canceling, making-someone-disappear because they've committed a perceived and grievous sin of humanity are abundant and almost always extreme. And if they're not extreme, they certainly feel that way.

You overexpose yourself, a writer friend once told me. I was complaining to her about something someone had said about me, and it had made its way back to me like the game of telephone.

You need to be more withholding, she added.

And maybe she's right. But, again, I believe—and this is something I teach my students early on—that no authentic character we create, *no person*, is all good or all bad (with some obvious exceptions). The story of my grandmother leaving her family was representative of profound human imperfection that begged the question *Why.* Vilified everywhere, she returned; this is the one piece of the story that is always conveniently omitted. Whether she found herself having to choose between a family or a life in music or was confronting a return to an abusive spouse or overwhelming postpartum depression, her story is one of acute flaw and utter humanity.

To wrap oneself in a veneer of flawlessness is to lead a lonely and inauthentic life; on the page—whether we are writing fiction or nonfiction—it results in a thin, one-sided narrative, devoid of truth and the beauty of our humanity, with all its frailties and foibles.

15

NOISE AND QUIET

True solitude is found in the wild places,
where one is without human obligation.
One's inner voices become audible.

—WENDELL BERRY

I WAS NEARING the end of the first complete draft of this book last spring, while on the writer's residency in Texas where I had previously met the turtle-loving vintage-shop owner. I had arrived there with a plan:

> Get up early.
> Go for a long walk.
> Come back to my space.
> Answer emails.
> Disconnect from social media.
> Write for four or five hours.
> Another walk.
> Dinner.
> Read.
> Sleep.
> 2,000 words a day.

I arrived in the high heat and humidity of early April; it couldn't be helped. Texas; climate change. Spring is the new Summer. The ancient, beautiful brick building I was staying in, an Oddfellows Hall that was at one time rented out to both the local Orthodox Jewish community and the Ku Klux Klan, not simultaneously, was from the eighteen nineties: no heat, no air conditioning. Normally, I am told, this was not a problem. It was ninety degrees in my studio when I arrived from the East Coast, which required the locating of a freestanding air conditioning unit and its installation on the other side of the dividing wall that separated my sleeping area from the hallway. The director of the residency was very kind and helpful, and provided me with a plastic tub for the condensation being spewed by the hose in the back of the machine; I had to empty it every three hours, even through the night, because of the humidity. Then there was the chair: my Scandinavian-style desk chair was highly fashionable, formed from bent plywood, and unsuitable for long spates of writing.

Once I got settled, I wrote from the bed, the floor, the coffee shop down the street, until on the third day I was no longer able to stand because the lumbar disc that I blew out writing my second book (bad chair) collapsed. The kind residency director gave me his chair, which was padded. I could write again for long periods and wake up the next morning upright, as opposed to bent over at a forty-five-degree angle.

My clothes swayed in my closet every evening until two in the morning. A Tex-Mex band with a heavy oompah bass line played around the corner until the middle of the night. The first time this happened during the first week of my stay, I lay awake, staring at the twenty-foot ceiling above my bed. I watched the sun come up in this small Texas town where I would be living and writing for a month.

I became unhinged. I was completely exhausted. I finally fell asleep until eleven in the morning and by the time I got myself together, it was noon, and half my day was gone.

The bass. A known problem, the director said. *Happens every Friday night. Usually, we just call the cops.*

On the third morning of my residency, my phone buzzed; my elderly mother couldn't figure out how to make a call on her cell phone. She was furious. She was screaming. I was screaming. I explained: *dial the number and press the big green button.*

Come home and fix it, she demanded.

I'm in Texas, I said.

So? she said.

Just shut your phone off and go somewhere else, a writer friend texted when I wrote to her, incensed. *Stop complaining. I don't want to fucking hear it.*

Neither did I; I did not want to hear anything, from anyone. I just wanted to work in quiet, which is why I was there.

We live in a distracting universe, by design. Work that requires intense concentration and focus, and often a stepping into memory and time as a way to reinhabit feeling and experience, is almost impossible to do with a pinging phone, email, social media. When I was writing my third book, I regularly worked in nearby libraries to escape the whining dog, the noisy neighbor, the demanding cats, the relentless phone. One afternoon, at a large and beautiful well-endowed library in a nearby town on the Long Island Sound, I sat myself down in a secluded carrel with my computer and my notebook and a chunk of my manuscript, and I began to work. Ten minutes later, a tall, immense man stood about a foot to my right and took a phone call on his cell: he put it on speaker so he didn't have to hold it up to his ear.

Excuse me . . . I said to him, incredulous.

What? he gasped. *Go someplace else. This is a fucking public space.*

And he was right; it was. But because I was alive when dinosaurs walked the earth, I have a vivid memory of libraries being places of silence and thought, where one might go to work in peace. When I was a Boston University undergraduate in the eighties, the Mugar Library was known as a pickup joint, so I began to study in the very quiet School of Theology Library, and I worked there regularly until I graduated.

I had expectations—assumptions, really—about this fancy library on the Sound, but I was wrong. I had asked permission from this nasty man with the cell phone that he respect the rules of the space—quiet—thus allowing me to write, and he told me to go to hell.

Didn't you know? a local writer friend of mine asked. *It's a terrible place for quiet.*

A few weeks later, Dani Shapiro, who lives nearby, generously passed along her office space—the place where she'd written her last book—in a tiny Litchfield County town. No Wi-Fi, no cell service, no noise, no nothing. Every morning I made myself a thermos of coffee and packed a bag containing my laptop and the chunks of manuscript that I was working on, and drove north to the tiny town of Washington Depot; I took a break during the midafternoon and went on walks along the nearby river. I returned to my home in the evening. And it was in that little office where I finally, eventually, finished my book.

Not every writer or artist is as lucky as I was, though.

You must be very rich to be able to afford an off-site office, one frenemy said to me. *Good thing you don't have to work for a living.*

In fact, I had been given permission—and the space (for which I was paying a pittance to the kind landlord)—to do my job, for which I *was* being paid. I considered explaining myself to deflect my friend's snarky comment; instead, I just let it sit. I chose not to fan the flames. I did not need her permission for my writing to be considered *real work*. I also did not need permission to require quiet in which *to do* my work.

No one does—not I nor you—and it is sometimes easy to forget this.

We live in a world that swings on the hinge of disruption, like an annoying, creaking door. Finding quiet in which to do one's creative work—whatever it is: writing, painting, throwing pots, composing—has been made virtually impossible by the pull of the dopamine hit, the built-in, addictive need to look at one's phone, to check one's email, to look at Instagram. Anna Lembke, the Stanford neuropsychologist and author of *Dopamine Nation*, puts it this way: *The smartphone is the modern-day hypodermic needle, delivering digital dopamine 24/7 for a wired generation.* So addicted to that hit of digital dopamine are we that app-blocking programs like Freedom have taken the creative world by storm, promising focus and productivity and the ability to turn off any, to quote their website, *distracting websites and apps.* I downloaded it when I was writing *Motherland*, and set it to lock down my computer for five hours at a time; by hour three, I was crawling out of my skin, desperate to check my email just to see if anyone was trying to reach me. All I had to do was pick up my phone, which I chose to leave unlocked, and open up my Gmail account.

This need-fulfillment—this biological compulsion for a fix—is noise just as much as the bass line that made my clothing sway in the residency's antique chifforobe in which it hung.

Noise can be internal; noise can be external; noise can be emotional. Noise is noise, and if noise is preventing you from living a creative life—and living a creative life is not a romantic notion; it is possible, and necessary for every one of us, and when we don't do it, it affects every other part of our lives—it will make you a slave to demand. It will turn you into an automaton. You will move through your days like a ball in a pinball machine. If one chooses to spend most of their creative energy on social media—on producing gorgeous, engaging TikToks, or Instagram posts designed to capture the attention of readers—then one is actively *choosing* noise and willingly opening the floodgates of distraction. Is it a form of art? Certainly. Does it take creative skill? Absolutely. Is there a place where overlap occurs—where, for example, poetry is born on the small screens of our iPhones? Definitely. Look at the work of people like Rupi Kaur or Diego Perez, otherwise known as Yung Pueblo.

For the rest of us, if the noise of social media takes over, then the grounding possibility of making art, in whatever form it exists for you, will become secondary, or even tertiary. Or it won't come at all because you will have not made space for it and given it the respect that it deserves. And if you did have space for it at some point, you freely gave it away.

Quiet, too, comes in all forms, be it literal or figurative. Quiet comes when your own inner critic stops yammering about the quality of your work, or stops comparing it to the work of others. Quiet comes when your demons are put to rest, and the voices of shame that say your story is too dangerous to be told or breaks an ancient code of silence or that no one will believe you are silenced. Quiet comes when you, having investigated your own motivations for writing about something dangerous, gingerly move forward.

Anne Lamott thinks of this literally, imagining the voices being connected to tiny, bug-eyed demons that she drops into a jar with a lid, screwing it on tight and letting them scream until they exhaust themselves, unable to be heard while the work gets done.

Quiet is the opposite of the assaultive thump of the bass player at two in the morning, and the pull of social media; quiet is the opposite of the person who tells you to *just get over it,* or that you're kidding yourself, or *who the fuck do you think you are*; quiet is the permission you give to yourself to make your art, even when the voices are howling with furious laughter that you're not very good, or you're a fraud, or that yours isn't a story you should tell because the memory of that upstanding member of your community—the teacher or maybe the swimming coach—who drove you to a secluded park every day after school will be besmirched.

Quiet is the permission you give yourself to tell your story when you've spent years being gaslit into believing that it never happened.

Quiet is the peace that you find when, after a day or a decade, a week or a month, you allow yourself to crack open the story that you must tell in order to find its pulsing heart, and to devote yourself to it and the crafting of it as art.

❧

Years ago, in the eighties, I had a roommate who was a modern dancer. After an injury ended her dance career, she went on to become a highly sought-after massage therapist and then a therapist specializing in EMDR: eye movement desensitization and reprocessing, a modality known to be successful in treating post-traumatic stress disorder, or PTSD. But between the time I met her, in 1987, and her becoming an EMDR therapist years later, she flung herself into a noise-quieting creative practice without even knowing it, as did anyone who picked up Julia Cameron's *The Artist's Way*, which began life as a self-published treatise on living a creative life before being published as a book some years later. *The Artist's Way* is known primarily for one key practice: morning pages, in which one sits down with a journal or notebook early enough that the brain and ego have not yet been kicked into gear, and writes three longhand pages, nonstop. What results is a stream-of-consciousness clearing of the muck that lives in one's head—the tumbleweeds of distraction, the low buzz of noise—allowing for a movement toward, as Cameron says, *creative, constructive action*. Morning pages are in no way subject to qualitative analysis or evaluation; they are meant only for the writer's eyes, and this is key. They are not meant to be workshopped, or published, or in any way shared.

Every day my roommate crept out of bed at sunrise before her day began, grabbed her notebook, turned the light on over the kitchen table, and wrote her morning pages. And little by little, month after month, this noise-reducing practice—this habit—began to herd her toward the work that she was most connected to after a career-ending injury forced her to change course and leave the dance world. She was able to quiet the noise of *You Should Do This* and *You Should Do That* enough to understand that she wanted to create a life that was *proactive* rather than *reactive*, that was not only a life of service to others but one that was always somehow touched by art-making, which was a non-negotiable for her. It didn't matter how many hours a day or weekend she spent in graduate school fulfilling course requirements; she was pulled to creative work. It was never a means to an end: she was a lousy painter. The lopsided mugs she threw at the local pottery studio could barely hold a cup of tea. But for every hour she spent hunched over books or working with clients, she spent at least a little time every day creating *something*, just for the sake of it. Art-making for the sake of art-making. The noise of *You should* was silenced by what Lewis Hyde in *The Gift* calls a *revival of the soul*; that is what art-making does.

*　　*　　*

When we were out hiking one day on Overlook Mountain in Woodstock, New York, and she cut a fistful of scraggly, dying cattails because she found their color and texture beautiful, my roommate carried them back to the cottage we were staying in as tenderly as she would have carried a baby, laid them out on dark brown artist's paper, and affixed them with floral tape. It was so lovely that we had it framed; it hung over our living room sofa until a few years later when we went our separate ways, a reminder that the making of art never has to occur for a specific reason. It is a uniquely human impulse, assuming we quiet our lives and our minds enough to do it and to honor it as vitally necessary for our souls.

I left the residency in Texas two weeks early because of the noise: the literal noise, the psychic noise, the relentless environmental chatter and distraction and thrum, the knowledge that I was going to have to battle it every day and every night for as long as I was there, and I was there to focus on my work. I apologized profusely to the kind residency director and meant it; I had to leave for the sake of my writing. I booked my flight home two weeks early. I spent the entire day after my arrival home in bed, asleep, making up for the lost sleeping hours. And then I went to a library—not the fancy one on the Sound—and got back to work and the business of quieting the noise, getting out of my own way, and staving off the perfectionism that is as natural to me as the color of my eyes.

16

SUCCESS

INTERVIEWER: *You mentioned getting permission to write. Who gave it to you?*
MORRISON: *No one. What I needed permission to do was succeed at it.*

I N A Fall 1993 *Paris Review* the Art of Fiction interview, Elissa Schappell spoke with Toni Morrison about the writing life. Morrison talked about writing while holding down a full-time job as an editor, writing with small children in the house, writing as a woman, writing as a woman of color, writing about controlling one's own characters (and not), and writing about sex (*It's just not sexy enough*). Morrison talked about the weapons of the weak, and how they impact the work of writing: nagging, poison, gossip. And about permission to write, and permission to succeed at it.

I read those words and had a sticky, squirmy reaction; I felt the way I do when I stand back and witness the horror of someone else's undoing. It's a tight kink in the stomach, a hard walnut in the throat. We've all been there: we've seen the speaker who loses the words, the young actor who blanks out on stage, the musician who forgets the chords. We recognize the writer—the food writer, the science writer, the academic, the novelist, the poet—blocked by fear. We wince. *Who are they to even try?* We whisper as we watch the artist tumble from their place. We look away; it's too hard to watch.

When it comes our time, we become that person, naked on the stage: doubtful, panicky, assured by the nagging, the poison, the gossipy gremlin chatter over our shoulder, promising us that someday we too will most certainly—definitely—fail.

A TEDx talk I gave in front of two thousand people: I practiced my twelve-minute talk for six months, memorizing it perfectly. There are no teleprompters at TEDx events; speakers rely only on their memories and passion for their subjects. Ten of us arrived at the location a few days early to acquaint ourselves with the stage, and each other. One of my fellow speakers—arrogant, haughty, generally rude—took great pleasure in laughing out loud at each of us while we rehearsed. There was an oncologist turned cancer patient. A queer Big Ten football player from a very red state. The widow of a mountain climber left to raise their children after losing her husband in an avalanche. The day of the event, the haughty speaker confidently strode out on stage and made it through three minutes of her talk before forgetting what came next; her face burned with shame and horror, and she walked offstage. She went back out a few minutes later, composed herself, and finished her talk. The theater erupted in applause. The rest of us watched, sipping a stiff cocktail of schadenfreude mixed with relief. Humanity at its most vile and its most supportive—two sides to the same coin. *Who does she think she is?* we asked, as we watched her stumble over her words. And then when she went back out onstage: a reprieve. There were tears—honest, authentic tears—and an explanation: she came from a family where women were meant to remain in the background, to raise their babies, to speak when spoken to. She had made it to the stage of a two-thousand-seat theater to talk about being a successful business owner in a family of naysayers when it hit her: no one had ever said *Go ahead. Tell your story. Succeed at your work. We give you permission.*

Some years ago, I left a full-time job I loved to write my second memoir, *Treyf.* Before I quit, I wrote on the train in longhand scribbles, at night in my pajamas, during lunch breaks, on the weekend, until it became clear to me that I had to step away from one job or the other. I was exhausted; I couldn't manage to do both. The decision was made: I relinquished my position tearfully. I loved it and was good at it—I had long since been given permission to succeed at being an editor—and I went home to my office and closed the door, and wrote.

I sat down to work every morning at eight thirty, and apart from doing yoga a few times a week, walking the dogs, and making myself endless cups of tea, I didn't move. Some days the work flowed like a river. Some days I stared at the page—each word I managed to eke out was like squeezing the back end of an elephant through the eye of a needle—and wept. Alone. I asked myself the same thing I had asked while I was writing my first memoir, eight lines of which destroyed my relationship with much of my family. Here I was again.

Do I have permission to succeed at this? Who am I to tell my stories, to call myself an artist, a creative?

Who are you not to tell them? a writer friend said to me.

This writer friend—author of novels, memoirs, a short story collection—tells me that it is ownership, and acceptance of the fact that our stories make us who we are, that is the most complicated and treacherous part of what we do. When that ownership is withheld, we cannot succeed. When other forces say, *No, that story is not yours,* they have not only killed it and its place in your soul; they have killed *you.*

There are plenty of hurdles in the art-making process: distraction, diligence, envy, arrogance, dedication, time, space, money, nagging, poison, gossip. One writer I know spends so much of her time curating her life on Instagram that she's left herself with virtually no time to work. There is the seductive conceit that lures you, like an animal into a trap, toward the belief that your work is spectacular, whatever that means, long before it is actually done. There's the quicksand of self-doubt, so immobilizing that you can neither climb nor claw your way out of it, and the more you struggle against it, the deeper you get sucked in.

The hurdles can make you think you're *better or worse than.* They can shut you down, prop you up, alter your course, tack your sails. They can result in moments of bliss and terror, calm and panic, hubris and humility, pomposity, paranoia, and paralysis. Often within moments of each other.

These obstacles may hinder permission to write, but they don't withhold permission to succeed at it. The rickety, splintering plank connecting the two, as quivery as a rope bridge over a gorge, is reserved strictly for shame.

You don't think shame, says Janna Malamud Smith. *You feel covered in its viscose grime. The great hand immerses you whenever you are told you are, or believe yourself to be, violating a basic communal code.*

Truth: A well-known food writer tells me that no matter what she writes—her blog, her cookbooks, her endless articles—she is filled with paralyzing shame. *My mother,* she tells me, her eyes filling with tears, *is the family cook. I was supposed to be the lawyer.* When she won her first cookbook award, her mother asked, *Who do you think you are?* Every time the writer sets pen to paper, she is overcome with guilt and anguish. Every recipe is poisoned with the pang of resentment. *I will never be a success,* she says to me. *It would kill her.*

Truth: An artist in her fifties has devoted her life to creating bright, colorful pencil drawings. *It's a nice hobby,* her elderly parents say, *but your sister is the real artist. Why didn't you become a teacher the way we hoped?* Forever mired in disappointment—hers, theirs—her images are the same ones she drew when she was eleven, stuck in time and place like their creator, longing for approval, waiting for the permission she will never receive.

Truth: A writer tells the story of something that happened to her late father almost a century earlier. The story, one of abandonment, is inherently cloaked in shame. Haunted by this family myth, which feels almost Greek, this writer and her worldview have been molded and shaped by it since she was a child. It forever transforms her sense of safety and self. She writes it and is expelled by her family, who kept it a secret for nearly one hundred years. *Who do you think you are to write about this?* they say.

Janna Malamud Smith writes: *Shame [is] a group survival reflex in which the individual is an afterthought. Shame's first goal is to have you conform to group expectations . . . One way art transforms shame is by replacing helplessness with agency.*

Like Toni Morrison, we look beyond ourselves for the permission to succeed. This external yearning for that which is granted by someone or something else—something outside us—is instilled in us from infancy and metabolized like mother's milk. *May I, can I, should I?* To disregard it is to step into a trap. To flout shame, to poke it in the eye, is to invite abandonment. As writers and artists, we depend upon the external to feed us after our solitary days at work. To violate that compact feels like sure death; in truth, it is life. This is where the magic begins.

Respect the story that you carry with you in your heart, that you must tell. Understand that no one will give you permission to write it. Instead, *listen* to what the story has to reveal to you.

Quiet the noise around you. Soften its pitch. Our deepest stories are our best teachers. Let the weapons of the weak—the poison, the nagging, the gossip—burn themselves to ash. Cast them to the wind. Take back the permission to tell your story, and to succeed at it. Make it yours.

17

NOLI TIMERE

I was afraid to write because I was ashamed of my feelings and beliefs. The practice of any art can be a good excuse for self-loathing.

—HANIF KUREISHI

I n my home office, I have two desks. The one I'm sitting at right now, where I am writing this on a laptop perched on top of a thick cookbook set upon a stand (because I am quite short), is an antique Irish pine behemoth facing a wall. Hanging on the wall above me is a linen-covered pinboard tacked with old photos, an invitation to contribute an essay to an anthology on shame, two index cards (one with the first lines of another essay I'm currently writing, about sexual fluidity in the seventies), a Cheryl Strayed quote about resilience in the writing process, and a yellowing piece of paper emblazoned with the last words of Seamus Heaney, which I also have tattooed on my left arm, just above my wrist: *Noli Timere*. Also on this desk: piles of paper, a modem, a router, a podcasting microphone, a small bookshelf, a black glass bottle that used to contain expensive California olive oil, a hardcover copy of Zadie Smith's *Feel Free*, my father's leather notebook from the thirties, the framed photo of my father's naval squadron that hung in his childhood bedroom in Brooklyn where I lived for two years in the nineties, and a massive light box because I live in New England, where winters are dark and long.

My other desk, which faces the window out to my backyard, is small and mission-style, dark oak, with a drawer that, when you pull it open, reveals a secret hinged box in which I keep things I've written that belong neither in my journal nor my manuscripts. I found this desk in an antique store in Soho many years ago, and for a long time it sat unused in our guest room until I decided to move it in here, under the window. It gets perfect light, and on it I keep my wife's late Uncle George's solid oak toolbox, its small drawers filled with original tools from the thirties, which, when they come and visit us, I will be giving to my dear friend, writer and artisan RF Jurjevics, adult child of the writers Laurie Colwin and Juris Jurjevics, and a polymathic talent who, when they are not writing, creates remarkable jewelry and small statuary with their hands. Perched on the toolbox is a tiny brass Ganesha, to remind me to get out of my own way (I also wear a tiny gold Ganesha charm around my neck, because getting out of my own way is a theme). The desk chair—different from the expensive, modern Aeron chair I'm sitting on as I write this—is my wife's grandmother's Windsor chair, from the early nineteenth century.

Two very different desks; two very different jobs. I teach from the Irish pine behemoth, do Zoom calls, write various commissioned pieces, put out daily eldercare fires, conduct business, organize taxes, pay bills. I write—by hand—at the little mission desk, facing out the window at a massive lilac tree that blooms every June, sending clouds of sweetness in through my open office windows on the summer breezes.

Years ago, I wrote anywhere, on anything, at any time. In the early nineties, I was briefly temping for a famous Manhattan advertising agency, and because I wasn't on staff, I spent a lot of time just sitting at my desk, reading anything that crossed my path. And because I had access to stacks of pads, I spent hours—literally, *hours*—writing by hand, until one of the people I worked for asked me to Xerox something for them, or get them coffee, or make them an appointment. Days often went by where my services weren't needed, so I read, or I wrote. When I was moved to another department, there were no pads available—it was just me and a phone—so I took to writing on the inside front covers of the paperbacks I was reading (I couldn't afford hardcovers), all over the frontmatter, all over the backmatter, and on the inside back cover; it's not something I'm particularly proud of. It never occurred to me to buy a notebook, and I have no idea why. I'd forgotten about this until recently, when I was in my basement in Connecticut and I opened a box, blew the dust off a dog-eared Natalie Goldberg book, and discovered my wild young scribbling all over its front and back pages.

One line on the title page reads, in my handwriting: *Who am I to write? Who do I think I am?*

At the time, I was living in my grandmother's Brooklyn apartment with all of her things—the opened box of Coffee Nips sitting on the foyer table; the false teeth in the medicine cabinet; the bags of letters and photos sent between my naval-aviator father and his parents and sister during World War II. I was surrounded by all of my family's old phantoms, and the stories and secrets that accompanied them.

It would be twenty-two years before my first book came out, before the familial excision that would change my life, and the time I would begin in earnest to question issues of creative permission and story ownership.

I was in my mid-fifties and the author of three memoirs when I discovered the old paperback book in my basement. What was troubling wasn't so much the fact that I was writing *in* the book itself or even on the notepads while at work on someone else's dime; it was the frantic and obvious *compulsion* that struck me. All the writing had the telltale signs of being stream of consciousness: nothing was erased, sentences flowed into each other like water, as though it was coursing downhill and picking up speed along the way. When I was living in my grandmother's apartment, where my father and aunt grew up after their mother's return and where the stories oozed from the walls and the floors and the old ornate Duncan Phyfe–style furniture, my scribbled writing took on a frantic, feverish air; wherever I turned in that apartment were totems of the past and reminders of what had transpired there, what was spoken of, and what was not.

Some of my discoveries were devastating: I realized while I was living there as an adult that there were no pictures of me anywhere in the apartment and hadn't been when I was a child. Perhaps I just hadn't noticed it because I was so small, and young children are not wired to look for that sort of thing. But if I had—if I had realized that I was effectively absent among photos of cousins and other grandchildren—I squirreled it away in my viscera: an *unthought known*. From my earliest days, I had been an invisible lurker, a listener, a fly-on-the-wall. A ghost among ghosts.

Time as much as stood still at 602 Avenue T, and living there for eighteen months was also like being creatively shot out of a cannon: my writing was furious and urgent, but entirely for my eyes only. I had the sense that writing about what I found in that apartment wasn't *safe*, and although I had been deposited there after a bad breakup, and although no one made any attempt to remove the physical manifestations of my family's complicated past, it was assumed that I would stay silent about it all. During the time that I lived there, I submitted and published nothing but the southern newspaper book review that my aunt corrected at a family party. In the manner that nearly every member of my family on both sides was a masterful and trained musician who chose not to pursue it professionally, we were also a family of storytellers and artists driven by narrative and myth, and expected to remain quiet.

I always figured you for a writer, my cousin Nina once told me over dinner years ago, when I was still in college. Her words were prescient; I was going to be the writer in this tribe of oral storytellers, and everyone knew it; I was not, however, given permission.

But every day at my office at the advertising agency, words poured out of me onto whatever paper they could find. Every day, I experienced a kind of creative interiority that is now often difficult to capture; instead, I have to work at it, cultivate it, respect it, form a moat around it. I've gone so far as to create a workspace meant specifically *for it*—the little mission-style desk with the Windsor chair facing the garden often goes uninhabited for this reason—like the baseball diamond in *Field of Dreams*: the work would come if I built a precious and sacred place for it to blossom. Of course, this is both a romanticized notion of what it means to be a working writer, and also a misconception. The making of art can happen anywhere, and it does, often unexpectedly. Even at a cheap desk in a busy advertising agency.

Humans are creatures of *doing* and *being* and productivity, and we always have been; this is nothing new. The Calvinist way; *idle hands.* I grew up in a family of worker bees. My wife's subsistence-farmer grandmother had ten children and took five-minute naps on her kitchen floor between chores. My mother worked during the day as a model and performed live as a singer at night, coming home at four in the morning, seven nights a week. My father, in his late fifties, considered driving a New York City taxi in order to make ends meet in the years before his divorce from my mother. Likewise, most writers and creatives who work at it professionally must knit together a patchwork of jobs to make a sustainable living, whether or not we have a book under contract: we teach, we ghostwrite, we edit, we write short pieces and reviews, we jury contests, we fill in gaps wherever we can. Some years are feast, and others, famine.

How many of my students are parents of young kids, holding down one or two jobs, and trying to chisel out a sliver of mental quiet to get to this place of interiority and focus? Many of them. But they already *are* creatives. We all are. There is not one human alive who does not have a connection to some creative endeavor, even though it may not be obvious.

The danger is, as I have said, lack of *time* to create; but the greater danger is distraction, and the addictive lure of comparison and competition—our phones allow us to see who is doing what, and where, and how, and *Likes* function as an indicator of success or failure and self-worth—that prevents us from going inward and closing the psychic door, quieting the noise, and giving ourselves permission to be there without judgement, hindrance, or dread.

When my father and aunt made the decision to leave my grandmother's apartment with everything in place when she died, they were, consciously or not, creating a repository of our history. No one could have known that I would someday move in and be surrounded not only by her things, but by the centuries-old stories that enveloped them. When I began to pack up for my move back to Manhattan, I told my father that I had found in the depths of my grandmother's closet some of his letters home from the navy, written when he was not yet twenty. I asked him if he wanted the letters back, and he said no—they were for me to keep; no clearer permission was ever given to me. A decade later, they were all in my hands—the ones from the Brooklyn apartment, and the ones I took possession of when he died in 2002—and I read them from beginning to end, along with my grandmother's responses. In every note and card from him were the words to his mother: *Don't be afraid.*

Noli timere.

ACKNOWLEDGMENTS

There is a long time in me between knowing and telling, wrote Grace Paley. Nothing could be a more accurate representation of my experience writing this book. The issue of creative permission turned my life upside down, entering my world unbidden and (frankly) unwanted more than a decade ago. Over the years, I have approached it from every possible angle until I found its core, and tried to unpack the universal truth behind why the creative world—mostly women—struggles with it: issues of shame, of knowing one's place as designated by the larger culture in which one lives, of owning a narrative and maintaining a party line are plaited together in such a way that they can be paralyzing unless they are faced directly, and transcended.

This book would never have existed had it not been for my students. Grateful thanks to them all, but especially Judith Newcomb Stiles, Kathleen Papageorgiou, Kathleen McKitty Harris, Danielle Joffe, Catherine O'Neill Grace, Maggie Kirsh, Melissa Giberson, and Erin Henry. I offer my profound gratitude to Truro Center for the Arts at Castle Hill; Barnswallow Books, Mary Jane Young, and the Lesher Family Foundation; Fine Arts Work Center in Provincetown; Kyle Hobratschk and the Corsicana Artist and Writers Residency; and Vermont Studio Center for offering me the time and space in which to work. Many thanks to the arts organizations and institutions that invited me to read sections of this book in its earliest form, and to lead workshops on memoir, permission, and storytelling, including College of William and Mary, Orion, Woodstock Bookfest, Fine Arts

Work Center and 24 Pearl, Maine Writers and Publishers Alliance, Rutgers Community Writing Workshop, and Maine Media Workshop.

To my generous friends and colleagues who inspire me every day with their work and their words: Katherine May, Anne Lamott, Maggie Smith, Debbie Millman, Sari Botton, Kathleen Yale, Dani Shapiro, Diana Henry, Kerri Arsenault, Alice Elliott Dark, Bonnie Friedman, Margaret Renkl, Billy Renkl, Kathleen Hackett, Laura McKowen, Rose Clark, Sara Jenkins. To those who have provided love, foundation, and unfathomable patience: Susie Middleton, Martha Frankel, and Myra Slotnick. Deepest thanks to my family of both blood and choice: Rita Hammer, the Schwartzes, Londons, Turners, Hopkins, Fiebers, Puchkoffs, Murphys, Latowickis, The Other Turners, Pennarolas, Watsons, Simón de Swaan, Sherry Sawyer, RF Jurjevics, Pam and Richard Brawn, Cynthia Barrett, Tara Barker, Caleb Ho and Jacqueline Church, Jeff and Lynn Sternstein, Marcia Lippman, Louise and Mark Carpentier, Stevie and Porter Boggess, Linda Wells. And to my late father, Cy Altman, for bravely and generously sharing his stories with me, so that we might transcend them.

My profound thanks to Joshua Bodwell, Celia Johnson, David Allender, Elizabeth Blachman, Brooke Koven, Spencer Fuller, Caroline Brink, Virginia Downes and the wonderful team at Godine Books for giving this book the best possible home, and to my wise and steadfast agents Christie Hinrichs and her team at Authors Unbound, Rita Berger, Adriana Stimola and everyone at Stimola Literary Studio.

To my love, Susan Turner: you are my garden, my air, and my light.

E.M.A.

2025

RESOURCES AND
FURTHER READING

Austin, Daryl. "What You're Saying When You Give Someone the Silent Treatment." *The Atlantic*, March 26, 2021.

Bayles, David and Orland, Ted. *Art & Fear: Observations on the Perils (and Rewards) of Artmaking.* Santa Cruz, CA: Image Continuum Press, 2001.

Berry, Wendell. *A Country of Marriage: Poems.* Berkeley, CA: Counterpoint Books, 2013.

Bollas, Christopher. *The Shadow of the Object: Psychoanalysis of the Unthought Known.* New York: Columbia University Press, 1989.

Brooks, Arthur C. "Whatever You Do, Don't Do the Silent Treatment." *The Atlantic*, March 21, 2024.

Cameron, Julia. *The Artist's Way.* New York: Tarcher, 1992.

Carver, Raymond. "Gravy." *The New Yorker*, August 21, 1988.

Chang, Victoria. *Dear Memory: Letters on Writing, Silence, and Grief.* Minneapolis: Milkweed Editions, 2021.

Chee, Alexander. *How to Write an Autobiographical Novel.* New York: Mariner Books, 2018.

Dederer, Claire. *Monsters: A Fan's Dilemma.* New York: Knopf, 2023.

Didion, Joan. *Slouching Towards Bethlehem: Essays.* New York: Farrar, Straus and Giroux, 2008.

Dillard, Annie. *The Abundance: Narrative Essays Old and New.* New York: Ecco, 2016.

Dillard, Annie. *Pilgrim at Tinker Creek.* New York: Harper Perennial Modern Classics, 2007.

Dillard, Annie. *The Writing Life.* New York: Harper Perennial, 2013.

Doty, Mark. "Return to Sender." *The Writer's Chronicle*, October/November 2005.

Dochartaigh, Kerri ní. *Thin Places: A Natural History of Healing and Home.* Minneapolis: Milkweed Editions, 2022.

Ellerby, Janet Mason. *Intimate Reading: The Contemporary Women's Memoir.* New York: Syracuse University Press, 2001.

Febos, Melissa. *Body Work: The Radical Power of Personal Narrative.* New York: Catapult, 2022.

Friedman, Bonnie. *Writing Past Dark: Envy, Fear, Distraction, and Other Dilemmas in the Writer's Life.* New York: Harper Perennial, 2020.

Gordon, Mary. *The Shadow Man: A Daughter's Search for Her Father.* New York: Vintage, 1997.

Gornick, Vivian. *The Situation and the Story: The Art of Personal Narrative.* New York: Farrar, Straus and Giroux, 2002.

Gornick, Vivian. *Fierce Attachments: A Memoir.* New York: Farrar, Straus and Giroux, 2005.

Hall, Donald. *Life Work.* Boston: Beacon Press, 2003.

Hampl, Patricia. *I Could Tell You Stories: Sojourns in the Land of Memory.* New York: W. W. Norton & Company, 2000.

Hirsch, Marianne. *The Generation of Postmemory: Writing and Visual Culture after the Holocaust.* New York: Columbia University Press, 2012.

Hirshfield, Jane. "Da Capo" from *Each Happiness Ringed by Lions: Selected Poems.* Northumberland: Bloodaxe Books, 2005.

hooks, bell. *All about Love: New Visions.* New York: William Morrow, 2018.

Howe, Marie: *What the Living Do.* New York: W. W. Norton & Company, 1999.

Hyde, Lewis. *The Gift: Creativity and the Artist in the Modern World.* New York: Vintage, 2007.

Jinpa, Thupten. *A Fearless Heart: How the Courage to Be Compassionate Can Change Our Lives.* New York: Avery, 2016.

Karr, Mary. *The Liars' Club: A Memoir.* New York: Penguin Books, 2005.

Kenyon, Jane. "Everything I Know About Writing Poetry" from *A Hundred White Daffodils: Essays, Interviews, the Akhmatova Translations, Newspaper Columns, and One Poem.* Minneapolis: Graywolf Press, 2000.

King, Stephen. *On Writing: A Memoir of the Craft*. New York: Scribner, 2000.

Lamott, Anne. *Bird By Bird: Some Instructions on Writing and Life*. New York: Vintage, 1995.

L'Engle, Madeleine. *Herself: Reflections on a Writing Life*. New York: Shaw Books, 2001

LeGuin, Ursula K. *Writings on Life and Books*. New York: Harper Perennial, 2019.

Le Guin, Ursula K. and Naimon, David. *Conversations on Writing*. Portland, OR: Tin House Books, 2018.

Lessard, Suzannah. *The Architect of Desire: Beauty and Danger in the Stanford White Family*. New York: Random House, 1997.

Lopez, Barry. "Sliver of Sky." *Harper's Magazine*, January 2013.

Lott, Bret. *Before We Get Started: A Practical Memoir of the Writer's Life*. New York: Random House, 2005.

Macfarlane, Robert. *Underland: A Deep Time Journey*. New York: W. W. Norton & Company, 2020.

May, Katherine. *Enchantment: Awakening Wonder in an Anxious Age*. New York: Riverhead Books, 2023.

May, Katherine. *Wintering: The Power of Rest and Retreat in Difficult Times*. New York: Riverhead Books, 2020.

Messud, Claire. *Kant's Little Prussian Head and Other Reasons Why I Write: An Autobiography in Essays*. New York: W. W. Norton & Company, 2020.

Millman, Debbie. *Why Design Matters: Conversations with the World's Most Creative People*. New York: HarperCollins, 2022.

Mitchell, Stephen. *Bhagavad Gita: A New Translation*. New. York: Harmony, 2007.

Moore, Honor. *The Bishop's Daughter: A Memoir*. New York: W. W. Norton & Company, 2008.

Morrison, Toni. "The Art of Fiction, Number 134." *The Paris Review*, Issue 128, Fall 1993.

Oliver, Mary. *New and Selected Poems, Volume One*. Boston: Beacon Press, 2004.

Oliver, Mary, and Tippett, Krista: *On Being* podcast, February 5, 2015.

Ozeki, Ruth. *The Face: A Time Code*. Amherst, MA: Restless Books, 2016.

Phillips, Jayne Anne. "The Writer as Outlaw." *The Washington Post*, October 15, 1994.

Rich, Adrienne. *Of Woman Born: Motherhood as Experience and Institution*. New York: W. W. Norton & Company, 2021.

Rilke, Rainer Maria. *Letters to a Young Poet*. Translated by M. D. Herter Norton. New York: W. W. Norton & Company, 1993.

Rubin, Rick. *The Creative Act: A Way of Being*. New York: Penguin Press, 2023.

Saunders, George and Naimon, David: *Between the Covers* podcast, January 14, 2013

Shapiro, Dani. *Inheritance: A Memoir of Genealogy, Paternity, and Love*. New York: Knopf, 2020.

Shapiro, Dani. *Still Writing: The Perils and Pleasures of a Creative Life*. New York: Atlantic Monthly Press, 2013.

Smith, Janna Malamud. *An Absorbing Errand: How Artists and Craftsmen Make Their Way to Mastery*. Berkeley, CA: Counterpoint, 2013.

Smith, Maggie. *You Could Make This Place Beautiful: A Memoir*. New York: Atria, 2023.

Strayed, Cheryl, "The Love of My Life." *The Sun*, September 2002.

Weller, Francis. *The Wild Edge of Sorrow: Rituals of Renewal and the Sacred Work of Grief*. Berkeley, CA: North Atlantic Books, 2015.

Westover, Tara. *Educated: A Memoir*. New York: Random House, 2022.

Williams, Kipling D. *Ostracism: The Power of Silence*. Guilford, CT: The Guilford Press, 2002.

Williams, Terry Tempest. *When Women Were Birds: Fifty-Four Variations on Voice*. New York: Picador, 2013.

Winterson, Jeanette. *Why Be Happy When You Could Be Normal?* New York: Grove Press, 2013.

Elissa Altman is the award-winning author of the memoirs *Motherland, Treyf, Poor Man's Feast,* and the bestselling essay substack of the same name. A longtime editor, she has been a finalist for the Lambda Literary Award, Connecticut Book Award, Maine Literary Award, and the Frank McCourt Memoir Prize, and her work has appeared in publications including *Orion, The Bitter Southerner, On Being, O: The Oprah Magazine, LitHub, The Wall Street Journal, The Guardian,* and *The Washington Post,* where her column, *Feeding My Mother,* ran for a year. Altman writes and speaks widely on the intersection of permission, storytelling, and creativity, and has appeared live on the TEDx stage and at the Public Theater in New York. She teaches the craft of memoir at Fine Arts Work Center, Orion, Maine Writers & Publishers Alliance, Kripalu, Truro Center for the Arts, Rutgers Community Writing Workshop, and beyond, and lives in Connecticut with her wife, book designer Susan Turner.

A NOTE ON THE TYPE

Our text is set in Granjon. This typeface is named in honor of Robert Granjon. He was the boldest and most original designer in his day. Between 1557 and 1562 Granjon printed about twenty books in types designed by himself.

However, it's neither a copy of a classic face nor an entirely original creation. George W. Jones 1924 Linotype revival of Granjon is actually closer in style to the original Garamond cuts. What holds true is the most pleasant and readable italic. Robert Granjon often set his own books inspired by the cursive handwriting fashionable of his time.

Book design and Composition by Brooke Koven